ROBERT PHILLIPS

Also available by Robert Phillips, Christian Henning, and Richard Guzzo

Golf: How to Consistently Break 90

Golf Fitness Training: Core to Score

Golf Fitness: Shed Pounds to Shave Strokes

Golf Fitness: 30 Yards or More in 30 Days or Less

ROBERT PHILLIPS

Golf: How to Break 90 in 42 Days or Less

ROBERT PHILLIPS

With

CHRISTIAN HENNING

RICHARD GUZZO

Copyright © 2015 by
Golf Aggressive Publishing LLP

All rights reserved,
including the right of reproduction
in whole or in part in any form.

ISBN-13:
978-1500668075

ISBN-10:
1500668079

DEDICATION

To golf, for every round I've played has blessed me with great memories enjoyed with old friends those just met.

Quick Fixes to the 5 Most Common Swing Faults of Golfers Who Can't Consistently Break 90...

Golf can be difficult to describe in words. If "a picture is worth a thousand words," a video may be worth a million words.

With that in mind, I got together with my friend Rich Guzzo – two-time defending club champion at The Hyatt Hill Country Resort and we shot a video explaining 5 of the most common faults for golfers who don't consistently break 90.

And more importantly, we included some simple drills to help any golfer eliminate these faults from their game so they can shave valuable strokes off their scores.

I'd also like to keep you updated as we discover more and better strategies and ideas for improving your golf game.

To claim your FREE video and to receive important updates, please visit:

http://golff.it/9042

Table of Contents

WELCOME	XV
INTRODUCTION	17
GOALS	19
A SIMPLE STRATEGY FOR BREAKING 90	23
6 CRITICAL GOLF SKILLS FOR BREAKING 90	25
CRITICAL GOLF SKILL #1: CONSISTENTLY 2-PUTT	27
PUTTING FUNDAMENTAL #1: RELAX!	28
PUTTING FUNDAMENTAL #2: STROKE THE PUTTER "THROUGH" THE BALL	28
PUTTING FUNDAMENTAL #3: DON'T BREAK YOUR WRISTS	29
PUTTING DRILLS TO HELP YOU DEVELOP THE PROPER "FEEL"	29
THE "CIRCLE OF CONFIDENCE"	31
THE "CIRCLE OF CONFIDENCE" DRILL	32
"LAG" PUTTING DRILL	38
HAVING TROUBLE WITH THE LINE?	39
"BACK HALF" PUTTING DRILL	40
DISTANCE CONTROL DRILLS	40
DISTANCE CONTROL DRILL #1	41
DISTANCE CONTROL DRILL #2: THE TOWEL DRILL	42
CRITICAL GOLF SKILL #2:	45
CHIPPING AND PITCHING THE GOLF BALL ON TO THE GREEN (AND NEAR THE HOLE)	45
PITCH SHOTS VS. CHIP SHOTS	45
DEVELOPING "FEEL" AROUND THE GREENS	46
CHIPPING DRILL	47
PITCHING BASICS	49
PITCHING DRILL	50
CRITICAL GOLF SKILL #3:	53
TURNING 3 SHOTS INTO 2	53
THE "HOLY GRAIL" DRILL	53
CRITICAL GOLF SKILL #4:	55
CONSISTENTLY HIT YOUR TEE SHOTS 200+ YARDS (AND IN PLAY!)	55

THE DRIVER SWING	56
THE BASIC GRIP	57
THE "QUIET BOTTOM" DRILL	64
A SIMPLE DRILL FOR HITTING 200+ YARD DRIVES … AND KEEPING THEM IN PLAY TOO!	66
COMMON FAULTS AND FIXES	70
COMMON FAULT #1: POWER ZAPPER #1 – THE REVERSE PIVOT	70
THE FIX: "HAPPY GILMORE" DRILL	71
COMMON FAULT #2: THE SLICER'S DELIGHT – OVER THE TOP	71
THE FIX: "OTT BLOCKER" DRILL	72
COMMON FAULT #3: THE "QUICK" HOOKER – FORE LEFT!!!	73
"HOOKER" FIX #1: THE SLOW MOTION DRILL (SLOW DOWN)	73
"HOOKER" FIX #2: THE "ITO" BLOCKER DRILL	74
COMMON FAULT #4: PLAYING BASEBALL (LINE DRIVES AND GROUND BALLS)	74
THE FIX: THE 1,001 DRILL	75
COMMON FAULT #5: CASTING (POWER ZAPPER #2)	77
THE FIX: THE "WHOOSH" DRILL	77
CRITICAL GOLF SKILL #5:	79
CONSISTENTLY HIT APPROACH SHOTS NEAR THE GREEN (ON THE GREEN IS EVEN BETTER)	79
THE "GAME CHANGING" IRON STRIKING DRILL	83
CRITICAL GOLF SKILL #6: PLAY SMART GOLF!	87
(KEEP THE BIG NUMBERS OFF YOUR SCORECARD)	87
YOUR "PERSONAL PAR"	91
THE GAME PLAN: HOW TO BREAK 90 IN 42 DAYS OR LESS	101
THE STRANGEST SECRET	113
MY COMMITMENT TO BREAK 90 WITHIN THE NEXT 42 DAYS	115
APPENDIX A: PROVEN 2-STEP GAME PLAN FOR BREAKING 90	117
APPENDIX B: QUESTIONS & ANSWERS	123
APPENDIX C: ANALYZING A ROUND OF GOLF	131
APPENDIX D: ASSESSMENT SHEETS	151
APPENDIX E: PRE-SHOT ROUTINE FORMULA	163

ROBERT PHILLIPS

WELCOME

Welcome! And CONGRATULATIONS on making the decision to break 90 in 42 days or less. That's just 6 short weeks away.

Is it really possible to break 90 that quickly? YES!

I'm as serious about helping you break 90 as you are about consistently shooting scores in the 80s. Unfortunately, I cannot do it for you. Your level of DEDICATION and COMMITMENT will go a long way in determining your success.

It's not going to happen by magic or osmosis. It only happens with the DEDICATION and COMMITMENT necessary to achieve your goal!

So the real question is how badly do you want to break 90? How serious are you about shooting 89 or lower? Are you willing to devote just 30 minutes per day to developing and honing the skills necessary to lower your golf scores? Only you can answer those critical questions.

Action takers tend to be the most successful people in the world – in business, in their personal lives, in their communities, and in life in general. You've taken the first action to break 90 by investing in this program; yet that's just the first step.

Don't stop now. Keep the momentum going by getting yourself familiar with the 6 critical skills you'll need to develop in order to consistently break 90. There's a good chance you already have some of these skills. Keep reading to find out in just a few pages.

And if you haven't yet mastered these critical skills, I'll share some simple practice drills in the following pages. Many of these drills can be practiced at home so there's no reason you can get started today – in just a few minutes.

INTRODUCTION

By taking the time to read this book you are demonstrating your interest in improving your golf game to a level of skill that will allow you to consistently break 90.

That will put you in the elite group of the best golfers in the world. Only about 1 in 5 golfers can regularly break 90 so by dedicating yourself to achieving this worthy goal you will be rewarded with a lifetime of lower golf scores.

Research has shown people who put their goals in writing are more likely to achieve those goals. It's like making a written contract with yourself and nobody wants to let themselves down.

So before we get to the 6 critical golf skills you'll need to develop, demonstrate your commitment and dedication to achieving your goal by putting it in writing.

ROBERT PHILLIPS

GOALS

Make a goal, put it in writing, and post it prominently. Say it with me right now!

I WILL Break 90 in 42 Days or Less!

I am COMMITTED to practicing 2 to 3 hours each week to developing the skills I need to consistently break 90!

I DEDICATE the next 42 days to improving my golf game and lowering my scores – starting today!

I WILL Break 90 in 42 Days or Less!

That wasn't so hard was it? Now write it down, post it on your refrigerator, tape it on your golf bag, make it the screen saver on your computer. Whatever it takes to see your goal in writing every day as a reminder.

And if you're really serious, tell all your friends and family about your goal. Post it on your Facebook page if you have one. Tweet it. Encourage people you know to ask you about your progress and hold you accountable.

It's only 6 weeks – 42 days. That's only 11.5% of a year or 1.15% of a decade. And if you live to the average of about 70, it's just a tiny fraction of your lifetime – 0.16%. And people are living a lot longer than 70 years these days too!

Yet in that short period of time, you could set yourself up to get more enjoyment out of this great game for the rest of your life. You're only 42 days away from shooting the lowest golf scores of your life – if you're seriously COMMITTED to achieving your goal.

And as you see your golf skills improve and your scores drop, you'll naturally want to practice more. And the more you practice the better you'll get. I'm really excited for you and sincerely appreciative that you let me lead you on this 6-week journey that will change your golf life forever!

If you've never broken 90 or can't break 90 on a regular basis, I know exactly where you are because the truth is that until a few years ago I couldn't break 90 consistently myself. So I've been in your shoes and I know how you feel because not long ago I was in the same position you find yourself in today.

However, I dedicated myself to improving my golf game. I read and studied dozens of golf books, highlighting the best tips. I watched the Golf Channel and applied the tips that made sense to me. I'd even take notes as I watched Michael Breed on The Golf Fix every Monday night.

And most importantly I played with golfers that were better than me – single digit handicappers that consistently broke 80! These guys were upset to shoot 82! So they knew a thing or two about breaking 90.

I watched how they played the game. I learned from them. And when they offered suggestions I listened. Be careful from whom you take advice… As a general rule, I only listen to golfers who are BOTH better than me AND know my game because we play together often. I'll share some of the best stroke reducing tips with you.

The exception would be a professional golf instructor. Occasionally I have played with a few that have offered helpful tips and suggestions. And since that's their profession I heed their advice.

I'll share a great tip on how to make sure you club head is square at address. People had told me my club head was closed at address and I stubbornly wouldn't listen – until this pro convinced me of it in about 5 seconds with one simple test. I've been hitting the ball straighter ever since.

Bottom Line: Don't take advice from hackers who can't break 90 themselves. Or you'll end up playing bad golf just like them!

I'm NOT a professional golf instructor so I don't speak in technical golf language that only golf professionals understand. I speak in English! And when I do use a golf-specific term like "over the top" I'll actually tell you what I mean instead of assuming you already know.

As for lessons, I took a few but I got frustrated because the instructors never seemed as serious about improving my golf game and lowering my scores as I was! It seemed like they were only interested in keeping me around as long as possible so they could collect more of my money!

I remember paying one old codger who said he played with Ben Hogan about $300 for a series of five lessons. I stopped going after the second lesson because it was a waste of time!

I'm not saying you should avoid professional golf instruction. I'm 100% certain that if you can find the right teacher, you'll benefit from the instruction. I just haven't had much luck finding the right teacher.

I may not be a PGA instructor, yet I have teamed up with a scratch golfer who is just as serious about helping you break 90 as I am. His name is Rich Guzzo. He's originally from Australia and now lives in San Antonio, Texas.

Rich played college golf in Oklahoma. And he's the reigning club champion at The Hyatt Hill Country Resort in San Antonio. So he knows a thing or two about breaking not just 90 but 80 too!

I'm qualified to help you break 90 because I consistently do it myself. I've whittled my handicap down to 12. I'm now consistently shooting scores in the low to mid-80. It's rare that I don't break 90 anymore and I've even broken 80 several times with a personal low of 77.

And as a current club champion golfer, a former college golfer, a scratch golfer, and a general golf junkie for life, Rich is exceptionally qualified to help you break the 90 barrier.

The Goal of this Program is to help you Break 90 as Quickly as Possible

Before we get started, let me be crystal clear about the goal of this program. My objective is to help you break 90 as quickly as possible. Period. That's it!

If you can already consistently break 90, congratulations you are in the top 20% of golfers, but this program is not for you. It's designed for the majority of golfers who can't break 90 consistently.

I've tried to make this program as simple as possible. For that reason, it is not full of technical golf jargon or mechanical swing thoughts. We'll leave those for another time – probably when you're ready to break 80 consistently.

This program is designed to develop the critical golf skills necessary to break 90 consistently. And it's much more than just a list of these skills. I'll share simple drills you can practice to develop and master these skills.

I'll cover tee shots and approach shots but anyone who knows anything about the game of golf will tell you, the best opportunity to reduce your scores lies in the short game.

That's why bulk of this program is about developing a short game that allows you to put the ball in the hole in as few strokes as possible. Don't worry, I'll cover tee shots, approach shots, and course management too but the main focus is on the real key to shooting lower golf scores and specifically to consistently breaking 90 – the short game.

If you'll commit to practicing about 30 minutes per day, I GUARANTEE that as you develop and hone these golf skills, your confidence will rise, your scores will drop, your enjoyment of the game will increase, and you'll probably win more money from your friends too!

You don't need to practice for 30 minutes every single day. You can practice for one hour 3 times a week or for 3 hours over the weekend. It doesn't matter when you get your practice time in, what matters is that you actually practice.

A SIMPLE STRATEGY FOR BREAKING 90

Let's start with the simple strategy. Before generals go to war, they have a battle plan. And before you go to battle with the golf course you should have a plan too.

Stepping up the first tee box without a plan is like getting in your car and driving with no particular destination in mind. Without a plan or a roadmap, who knows where you'll end up? However, chances are you'll end up with a score north of 90.

Before I explain the simple strategy, let me say that I don't believe in any "one-size-fits-all" plan. Yes, there are certain fundamentals of golf that you must follow, yet we're all different.

Some golfers are long-hitters while others are short-knockers. Some players using long putters while others prefer short putters. There are multiple grips you can use both with putters and with your regular clubs. And yet even at the professional level, all different types of players with different styles of play win major championships.

The key is finding what works best for YOU! That concept applies throughout the next 42 days as we work together to lower your golf score and help you break 90.

How to Play One Stroke Better than Bogey Golf

Most golf courses have a par of 72 so that's what we'll work with. If your home course is set up like normal, you'll be playing 4 par 3's, 4 par 5's, and 10 par 4's for a total of 18 holes. Par every hole and your score is 72.

Here's the simple strategy for breaking 90. Play one stroke better than "bogey golf." In other words, if you bogey every hole you will shot a score of 90. So all you need to do is shoot one shot better than that to break 90.

Simple? Sure, but a lot easier said than done for most golfers. However, when you develop a few critical golf skills, breaking 90 will be a breeze.

ROBERT PHILLIPS

6 CRITICAL GOLF SKILLS FOR BREAKING 90

Critical Golf Skill #1: Consistently 2-putt (Minimize three-putts)

Critical Golf Skill #2: When you miss the green in regulation, pitch or chip the golf ball onto the green (the first time – and of course the nearer the hole the better!)

Critical Golf Skill #3: Turn 3 shots into 2 (The golfer's "holy grail")

Critical Golf Skill #4: Consistently hit your tee shots 200 yards or more AND keep them in play! (300-yard drives into the woods won't help you lower your scores.)

Critical Golf Skill #5: Consistently hit approach shots near the green (on the green is even better) and eliminate "mis-hits" like "fat" shots and "thin" shots.

Critical Golf Skill #6: Keep the big numbers off the card (Play Smart Golf!)

I've numbered these skills roughly in their order of importance. In other words, consistently two-putting most greens is the most critical skill while smashing the ball off the tee is a distant fourth – after the more critical short game skills.

None of these skills requires extraordinary strength or athleticism either. All that's required is the commitment and dedication to the regular practice that will help you develop these skills.

When you develop the first 5 "playing" skills, you'll have little trouble keeping the big numbers off the card. However, you'll still need to play smart on occasion so it's still a critical "mental" skill for lowering your scores.

It's interesting to note that most players who can't consistently break 90 spend far more time hitting drivers at the practice range than they do practicing their short game. While better golfers tend to spend more time honing their short games and less time pounding balls at the driving range.

This is NOT a coincidence. The simple fact is that improving your short game is the real key to breaking 90 consistently. Think about it. How many times have you hit a decent drive and a decent approach shot only to chili dip your pitch or three-putt or maybe even both?

If you can't consistently break 90, these common golfing mishaps probably happen more frequently than you either realize or care to admit. Sure the farther you can bomb your drives and the more accurately you can hit your approach shots the better, but it doesn't matter if you don't have a strong short game that allows you put the ball in the hole in as few strokes as possible.

However, a player who's merely average off the tee and average with his approach shots can still consistently break 90. If you can advance the ball near the green in regulation and then consistently pitch or chip the ball on to the green and two-putt, you're almost guaranteed to break 90. Simple as that.

What I'm trying to hammer home is that most people think about golf backwards. And for that reason they focus their practice on improving the areas of their game that don't matter as much – namely hitting long drives.

If you'll transform you're thinking and focus your efforts on the short game, it will go a long way towards lowering your scores. I'm going to give you more explanation on each of these critical skills, give you practice drills to develop these skills, and goals to make sure you acquire these skills.

Your goal should be to develop these critical skills and then improve upon them with particular emphasis on the short game. The most critical skill to develop if you're serious about regularly breaking 90 is…

CRITICAL GOLF SKILL #1: CONSISTENTLY 2-PUTT

Without a doubt, this is the most critical skill you need to develop. Sure it's nice to bomb drives and hit long irons but it won't matter unless you can put the ball in the hole! The "short game" is where you shave strokes and lower your score.

Yet for some reason, people most golfers spend the majority of their time whacking drivers and 5-irons at the driving range and precious little time on the putting green. It's backwards! And it's a big reason why most golfers can't consistently break 90.

Think about it. If you can two-putt every green, that's 36 putts over 18 holes. That gives you 53 more shots to play with. 18 tee shots. 14 approach shots (so as not to double count the 4 tee shots on par 3s). 4 fairway shots on the par 5s.

That's another 36 shots for a total of 72 – which still gives you 17 shots to play with. So you can miss 17 greens and as long as you can chip or pitch the golf ball onto the green and two-putt you'll still break 90.

That's the importance of the short game. Seriously if you can whack a 200+ yard drive and keep it in play, then slap an iron somewhere up near the green, all you have to do is chip or pitch the ball on to the green, then two-putt for bogey. One par and you'll break 90!

How do you think I know this? From personal experience – that's how I started breaking 90. I was decent off the tee – probably 240+ consistently. And even though my iron game was lacking to say the least, I could slap an iron shot up near the green.

And then I could pitch or chip the next shot on the green and two-putt for bogey. Sometimes I'd even put my iron shot on the green and two-putt for par or I'd get "up and down" for par from off the green. It was all about saving strokes with the short game.

Note: "up and down" is a common golf term that means you parred the hole despite missing the green in regulation because you got "up" (meaning you pitched or chipped the ball onto the green) and then you got "down" (meaning you made the putt).

So let's talk about putting and more specifically how to improve your putting to the point where you are consistently two-putting most greens. If you're wondering about putters and putter grips, I believe that's largely a personal decision. For more thoughts and suggestions, please see the Q&A section below.

Let's move on to actually holing more putts. I'm not going to get into the mechanics of the putting stroke for several reasons. First, I'm not a teaching pro. Second, it's difficult to describe in words (video is a much better way to see the proper technique). And third I don't believe in "one-size-fits-all" solutions. I believe it's your responsibility to figure out what works best for YOU.

However, there are a few fundamental thoughts I can share.

PUTTING FUNDAMENTAL #1: RELAX!

Tension is the enemy in golf. Don't hold the putter with a "death grip." Think about holding a small bird in both hands. You'd want to hold it firmly enough that it can't get away yet not so firmly that you squeeze it and crush it to death. That's a good thought when it comes to gripping a golf club.

Some people like to think of the grip pressure in terms of a scale of 0 to 10 with 10 being a tension-filled "death grip" and 0 being such a light grip you can barely hold the club at all. If you prefer to think of the grip this way, then try using a grip pressure of 3 to 4 – a relaxed grip yet firm enough that the club doesn't move in your hands in such a way that causes the putter face to wiggle away from being square at impact.

The majority of golfers who don't consistently break 90 grip the club too tightly. Loosening your grip will help you develop better "feel" and probably give you more power too.

PUTTING FUNDAMENTAL #2: STROKE THE PUTTER "THROUGH" THE BALL

Stroke the putter "through" the ball, not "at" the ball. When you stroke the putter "at" the ball, your muscles naturally become tense and that's not good (see putting fundamental #1). Stroke the putter "through" the ball. I have some drills to help you develop the proper "feel" of putting.

PUTTING FUNDAMENTAL #3: DON'T BREAK YOUR WRISTS

The putting stroke is not a wristy stroke. You should utilize the big muscles of the back and shoulders – not the small muscles of the fingers, hands, and wrists.

A good way to develop this technique is think of the triangle formed by your two shoulders and the putter head when you address the putt. Keep this triangle in place throughout the putting stroke. Think of it like the movement of a pendulum back and forth. The only way to break the triangle is to break your wrists.

PUTTING DRILLS TO HELP YOU DEVELOP THE PROPER "FEEL"

These drills will help you develop the proper "feel" of putting. They'll help you stroke the putter "through" the ball, not "at" the ball. The way you do it is by taking your eyes off the ball. Since you won't see the ball as you're stroking the putt, you'll avoid the natural tendency to tense up your muscles as you're about to make contact with the ball.

There are two ways to do this. The first way is to simply **close your eyes**. Take your normal putting stroke but as you start the stroke by taking the putter back away from the ball, close your eyes. Now finish the stroke as you normally would except don't open your eyes until after you've stroked the putt.

You should notice that it feels different when you stroke the putter "through" the ball instead of "at" the ball. The putt may roll a bit further too. That's because there's less muscle tension – preferably no muscle tension – when you stroke the putter "through" the ball.

The second way to develop the proper "feel" of stroking the putter through the ball is to **look at the hole instead of the ball**. So instead of looking at the ball, look at the hole and then stroke your normal putt.

Again, this takes your eyes off the ball and reduces the natural tendency for the muscles to tense up as you're about to stroke the putt.

These are practice drills only. They'll help you develop the proper "feel" for putting. I don't recommend you putt like this during your round.

Although, I've heard one of the best golfers on the LPGA tour – Suzann Petterson – actually has closed her eyes while putting in some LPGA tour events. Even the pros know the importance of developing the proper "'feel" in their putting stroke.

Calibrate Your Distances

Once you develop the proper "feel," you can calibrate your distances. You do this by stroking putts with gradually larger arcs and keeping track of how far the ball rolls. It shouldn't take long to figure out the proper stroke for a 5-foot putt, a 10-foot putt, a 15-foot putt, and a 20-foot putt.

It could be that your 5-foot putt is stroked by taking the putter 3-inches back of the ball and 3-inches forward of the ball after you stroke it. A 4-inch arc may produce a 10-foot putt. And 5-inch and 6-inch putting arcs may produce putts of 15 and 20 feet respectively.

Each golfer will be different so the lengths the putting arcs required for you to stroke 5, 10, 15, and 20-foot putts may be different than the example above. When calibrating your putting distances you don't need to putt at a hole. Just stroke the putt and keep track of the distance.

And you don't need to be so technical as to be thinking about making a 5-inch putting arc to stroke a 15-foot putt for example. Yet if that works for you and helps you putt, then it's OK to have that thought.

However, over time, the more you practice the more you'll develop a natural feel for what length putting stroke produces the proper distance. Practice these drills until you develop a good "feel" and are reasonably comfortable with your distance control.

Now that you know how to develop the proper "feel" for putting let's move on to actually sinking more putts. For the purposes of this program, there are two types of putts:

Putt #1: A "circle of confidence" or "COC" putt

This is a putt you expect to make – and you will make it most of the time. You stroke this putt confidently and aggressively. Your expectation is that after you stroke this putt, you'll reach down, pull your ball out of the cup, and move on to the next tee.

An example would be a tap-in from a few inches. You don't waste much time with the line and the speed. This is not a tentative "I hope it goes in" putt that barely trickles into the hole on the last roll. This is a firm, confident "knock the ball into the back of the hole" putt.

THE "CIRCLE OF CONFIDENCE"

If you're going to break 90 consistently, you really should be confident that you'll make most putts of 3-feet or less. When you are confident in your ability to hole every three-foot putt, you're in a good position to two-putt most of the time. All you have to do is stroke the first putt within a three-foot circle around the hole.

I call this your "circle of confidence." It's a simple yet very important concept. What's your "circle of confidence"? Here's an example. Let's say you're confident
you'll sink putts of 3 feet or less most of the time. In that case you would imagine a 3-foot circle around the cup and that would be your "circle of confidence."

If you're confident putting from 4-feet and in, then your "circle of confidence" would be a 4-foot circle around the cup with the hole being in the middle. So golfers with confidence from longer distances have larger "circles of confidence."

And it logically follows that the larger your "circle of confidence" is, the more likely
you are to 2-putt. So the first thing you must do is figure out the maximum distance from which you will make a confident and aggressive putting stroke and honestly expect to make the putt about 90% of the time. In other words, you'll sink 9 out of 10 putts inside your "circle of confidence."

Ultimately your goal should be to make every putt within a 3-foot radius of the hole. Of course, you'll occasionally miss a short putt – after all even PGA pros miss short putts once in a while. Yet you should reach a point where you have the confidence that you will hole every putt within a 3-foot radius of the hole.

So we'll start with the goal of creating a three-foot "circle of confidence" around the hole. And when you reach that goal, you can work on increasing the size of your personal "circle of confidence."

THE "CIRCLE OF CONFIDENCE" DRILL

Here's a simple drill for developing confidence and even increasing your "circle of confidence." The best part is that you can practice this drill either at the course or at home so there's no excuse for not improving your putting. And you don't need any special equipment or expensive gadgets either.

Measure out a distance of 3 feet at several points around the hole. If you don't have a tape measure don't worry. You should know approximately what 3 feet is; most standard putters are about 36 inches – 3 feet – in length. So if nothing else use your putter as a rough measuring tool.

Place four to eight balls around the hole to form a circle around the hole. This is your three-foot "circle of confidence." Now stroke each of these putts and keep track of how many you make. Remember, tracking your results is the best way to measure improvement.

As your results improve, you'll gain confidence in your putting, a positive attitude about your golf game, and if you're like most people, the better you get the more you'll want to practice to keep improving.

Some people like to line up their putts and some don't. Personally I do prefer to line up my putts. There are many ways to line up a putt and I recommend you use the way the works best for you.

Here's what works for me: I use a marker to draw a straight line on the ball. Then I line that line up with the hole. I also like to use putters with lines on them. That way I can make sure the line on the golf ball and the line on my putter are straight.

With few exceptions, you're playing a "circle of confidence" putt as a dead straight putt and you're slamming it straight into the hole. The only exceptions would be extremely fast greens with a lot of break. And frankly, you shouldn't be playing courses with greens that difficult until you can break 90 consistently on easier courses.

Remember, putts stroked inside your "circle of confidence" ("COC") are not at all tentative. It's a confident stroke you're expecting to make. That being the case, it's an absolute golfing sin to leave any of these putts short.

These putts should not be losing speed and trickling into the cup. That's what "lag putts" are for – we'll cover "lag" putts next. "COC" putts should hit the back of the cup with enough speed to roll about 18 inches past the hole on the rare occasion you happen to miss.

The reason for this is simple. The more speed on a putt, the better it holds its line. In other words, the more pace on a putt, the straighter it rolls. In most cases you ought be able to stroke a short three-foot putt dead straight right into the hole.

Being tentative and stroking the putt with less pace allows all sorts of bad things to happen. You could either leave the putt short or you could allow subtle breaks in the green to make you miss the putt to the left or the right. As it loses speed, a putt is also more likely to be affected by spike marks, ball marks, and footprints around the hole.

This is not called your "circle of confidence" for no reason. You know you're going to make these putts almost every time. That being the case, stroke the putt with confidence you're going to sink it.

Think about stroking the putt with enough pace to go 5 feet. The more you practice, the more you'll develop the natural feel for a putt that goes 5 feet. This pace will ensure the putt has enough speed that it shouldn't be affected by any spike marks or footprints around the hole.

And when you occasionally do miss, you'll have a short 2-foot putt on the way back. However, don't think about that. No negative thoughts allowed! You're going to sink 90% or more of these putts so putt with aggressive speed and confidence.

If you're not currently confident you're going to sink every putt within a three-foot radius of the hole, no problem. It takes practice and the point of this drill is to help you develop that confidence.

Keep your eye on the ball through impact. This is another important point. Don't take a "sneak peek" at the hole. Lifting your head before impact causes all kinds of problems so don't do it. Resist the natural urge to want to see where the ball goes before you hit it.

Here's a true story that helped me sink 3-foot putts. I was playing with some single-digit handicappers in a golf league. Playing with good golfers is probably my favorite strategy for getting better because you can learn so much.

Anyway, on the 7th green my friend Chuck who is a 5-handicapper told me I was peeking at my putts. He told me to just keep my head down and I'd make more of these 3-foot putts.

And you know what? I took his advice and I did not miss a single short putt the rest of the round. I resisted the urge to take a peek before impact. It was a bit of a challenge but it got easy fast because I started sinking all my short putts!

If you're having trouble with the "peeks," try this. Instead of using your eyes for feedback, use your ears. In other words, don't watch the ball go into the hole, listen for it. This is a great way to train yourself to keep your eyes on the ball through impact. And more importantly, it will prove that you'll sink more putts by not peeking!

If you're still peeking, force yourself to count before allowing yourself to look at the ball. Stroke the putt, then count "one-thousand-one, one-thousand-two." Only then can you lift your head and look at the ball.

Improve your "circle of confidence" at home...

You can work on your "circle of confidence" even if you can't make it to the course. You can easily do this drill from home. I like to use a sturdy ceramic coffee cup as the hole, then line balls up in a three foot circle around it.

Then you can walk around and stroke the putts keeping track of how many you make. I like using a sturdy ceramic coffee cup (placed either right-side up or upside down – NOT on it's side so balls can roll into it) for several reasons.

First, it's about the same size as a real golf hole. Actually probably a bit smaller which is good because if you can consistently hit the coffee cup from three feet then you certainly ought to be able to hit the hole on the golf course.

Second, a sturdy ceramic coffee cup won't budge when the golf ball collides with it at a good pace (remember, these are confidently stroked putts that hit the back of the hole with good pace!). If I were using a plastic cup, I would constantly have to put it back in place – no fun at all!

And finally, the ceramic coffee cup provides the audio feedback I like so that I can keep my eyes on the ball through impact. When I hear the clink of the golf ball hitting the coffee cup I know I've sunk the putt. I don't need visual feedback so there's no need to peek.

If you're having trouble consistently sinking 3-foot putts, don't worry. With some diligent practice I'm confident you'll quickly be sinking almost all of your putts inside 3-feet.

If you find you are consistently missing the putts either left or right, check your alignment and make sure you're lined up correctly. If you think you're lined up correctly and you're still not making the putts, you can use two golf clubs or two alignment rods to correct the issue.

Just line the clubs or the rods up with the hole, then practice stroking putts. If your putts are offline, the golf ball will hit the clubs or the rods. Adjust your aim until you can sink the putts without hitting the clubs or the rods.

If you're still having trouble, then most likely your putting stroke is not straight back and straight through. You're putting across the ball either from inside to outside which means you're probably "pushing" your putts to the right (and hitting the club or pole on the right – if you're a right-handed golfer).

Or you're cutting across the ball from outside to inside which means you're probably "pulling" your putts to the left (and hitting the club or pole on the left – again if you're a right-handed golfer).

You could also be manipulating the club face open (which would cause you to "push" putts to the right) or closed (which would cause you to "pull" putts to the left). Either way, it ought to be simple to figure out the flaw in your putting stroke and then fix it.

Developing the confidence that you're going to sink every putt from inside three-feet is a critical golf skill that will go a long way to helping you consistently break 90. The "circle of confidence" drill is designed to instill that confidence in you.

Practice this drill until you're confident you'll make every putt inside a three-foot "circle of confidence." And track your results to prove it! Every time you practice this drill, keep track of the number of putts stroked versus the number of putts holed. This is the only way to track your result and measure your improvement.

With that being said, here's the goal I recommend each week.

Sink at least 100 3-foot putts every week. This may sound like a lot, yet it only takes a few minutes to place 8 golf balls in a three-foot circle around the hole or around a ceramic coffee mug if you're practicing at home.

And as a shortcut, you could just place a marker down 3 feet away from the hole and stroke 10, 20, or more putts from that spot. Then move on to another spot and repeat the process. It shouldn't take long to stroke a hundred putts and develop confidence as your putting skill improves.

You could take an hour or so and sink all 100 putts at one-time. If you prefer you could sink 20 putts Monday through Friday. You could sink 100 putts over the weekend – 50 on Saturday and another 50 on Sunday.

You could stroke putts at home while you're watching TV – even if it's just on commercial breaks. When you do it doesn't matter as much as actually sinking 100 putts, tracking your results, measuring your progress, seeing improvement, and ultimately developing the confidence that you're going to hole every 3 foot putt inside your "circle of confidence."

You'll know you're getting better as you see the number of putts it takes you sink 100 drop. For example, the first week it may take 150 putts to sink 100. The next week you may improve to 130, then 115.

When you get the number down to 111 – in other words when you can sink 100 out of 111 3-foot putts – congratulate yourself because you're making greater than 90% of your putts and you now officially have developed critical golf skill #1. You have a 3-foot "circle of confidence."

You can also simulate the pressure of a real round of golf by setting goals. You could set a goal of making 10 putts in a row or maybe 4 out of 5. That's up to you. Just make sure the goal is challenging.

As you get close to achieving the goal, you should start to feel pressure. If your goal was to sink 10 consecutive putts, you'll probably feel more pressure to make the last 2 or 3 putts than you did on the first 7 or 8.

That's good because it teaches you how to deal with the pressure you'll feel out on the course during your round. When you've developed this critical golf skill, you've taken the first step towards consistently breaking 90.

So now let's move on to the second type of putt.

Putt #2: A "lag" putt

The goal of a "lag" putt is to get the ball as close to the hole as possible so that the next putt is inside your "circle of confidence" and preferably a tap-in. It's not an aggressive putt, you're just trying to putt the ball on the appropriate line with enough speed so that it stops inside your "circle of confidence."

Preferably your putt will have enough speed to roll past the hole (that way you'll actually sink some of these "bombs" once in a while) but there's nothing catastrophic about leaving a "lag" putt a foot or two short because you can easily tap-in for a 2-putt. You don't expect to hole a "lag" putt although sometimes you will. And if you do, that's a bonus.

The distance of a "lag" putt could be different depending on the golfer but for someone who can't break 90 consistently (at least not yet!), the distance should be in the 15 to 20 foot range. To start, we'll say lag putts are any putts greater than 15 feet. As your putting skills improve, increase the distance.

This is a good place to talk about reading greens. Reading greens is an important skill you'll develop over time but here are some simple tips that will help you read greens.

This is not always the case, but greens generally slope from back to front. That means the back of the green is higher than the front of the green. Greens are designed with a slope so the water runs off them when it rains.

That being the case, a putt from "below the hole (in front of the hole if you're standing on the front of the green) will be a slower, uphill putt that you'll need to stroke more firmly. And a putt from "above" the hole (in back of the hole if you're standing on the back of the green) will be a faster, downhill putt that you'll need to stroke less firmly.

Likewise a putt from the left side of the hole (looking at it from the front of the green) will break from left to right because the green will be sloping down to the right when putting from that direction.

And a putt from the right side of the hole will break from right to left because the green will be sloping down to the left when putting from that direction.

Remember, though, these are general guidelines. Not all greens slope from back to front. It shouldn't be difficult to take a look at the green as a whole and figure out which side of the green is noticeably higher and which side of the green is noticeably lower. From there you can figure out which way putts should break.

"LAG" PUTTING DRILL

To develop your "lag" putting skill, here's a simple drill. Pick a distance 15-feet or longer and stroke 10 putts from that distance with the goal of leaving them all within a 3-foot "circle of confidence" around the hole.

Again, set a challenging goal and don't stop until you reach your goal. If you're just starting out, your goal may be to leave 5 of the 10 putts inside your "circle of confidence."

If you've been practicing and improving your skill level, maybe your goal will be to leave 9 of the 10 putts inside the circle of confidence. Or maybe even all 10.

Not only does this provide a challenge that makes practicing fun, it also simulates the pressure of putting during a real round of golf. If you're down to your last putt and you must make it to achieve your goal, that's pressure similar to what you'll experience during your round of golf.

There are two ways to make this drill even more fun and more challenging. First you could make yourself sink the second putt. So your goal now could be for example, to stroke 10 putts leaving 8 of them inside a 3-foot "circle of confidence" and then sinking all 8 of those second putts.

Or you could shrink the "circle of confidence." I recommend cutting the COC in half to an 18-inch circle around the cup. So the goal now would be perhaps to stroke 10 putts and leave 6 of them inside an 18-inch "COC" around the hole.

The goal you set is up to you. The important thing is that it's a goal that challenges you based on your skill level. And when you reach the goal, raise the bar by setting a more challenging goal. That's how you'll improve your skill level and develop the putting skills that will help you break 90 consistently.

Depending on the layout of your home or apartment, if you have enough space, there's no reason you can't practice this drill at home.

HAVING TROUBLE WITH THE LINE?

If your distance control is good but you're having trouble with the line – in other words your putts are stopping to the left or right of the "COC" – you could use clubs or alignment rods to help. Position a club or rod in such a way that the ball must roll above it to be on the proper line.

To make this even more challenging, you could use two clubs or rods and position them in such a way that the ball must roll through them without touching them.

The closer the clubs or rods are positioned – in other words the narrower the alley for the ball to travel though – the more challenging it is to not hit the clubs or rods. This is quite challenging. However, if you can do this, you're a good putter!

This is really simple. However if it sounds confusing, please watch the video that shows this simple drill. Now let's move on to the final type of putt…

How to hone your putting skills even further!

One you can consistently "lag" putt inside your "circle of confidence," you can improve your putting skills even more by eliminating the front half of the "COC" leaving only the "back-half" of the "COC."

I sometimes call these "back-half" putts because if you miss this putt you want it to have enough pace to stop in the "back-half" of your "circle of confidence." That's the goal.

That's because putts of say 15-feet or less are definitely makeable so you should strive to NEVER leave a "back-half" putt short. In other words, you're eliminating the front-half of the "circle of confidence." You'll be amazed at how many of these putts you'll sink if you'll just get them to the hole!

There's nothing more frustrating than having your putt dead on line only to see it screech to a halt a few revolutions before dropping into the cup. And as an added benefit, not only will you sink some of these putts when you stop leaving them short, since they'll roll past the hole you'll be able to see any dramatic break as the ball rolls past the hole. You can then use that knowledge to sink the next putt.

"BACK HALF" PUTTING DRILL

Practice this drill from various distances: 5 feet, 10 feet, and 15 feet is a good start. Stroke putts from these distances with the goal of sinking the putt. However, if you don't sink the putt, stroke with the pace that leaves it in the back half of your "circle of confidence." NEVER leaves these makeable putts short!

Set a goal and don't stop until you achieve it.

The goal could be different from various distances. For example, perhaps from 5 feet you may set the goal of stroking 10 putts in a row that you either sink or leave in the back half of your "COC." From 10 feet perhaps the goal is 8 of 10 and from 15 feet, 7 of 10.

The goal you set is a personal decision based on your skill level. Just make sure it's a goal that challenges you. And as you achieve the goal, set a more challenging goal the next time you practice.

Again, this will simulate the pressure of a real round of golf. When you have two putts left and you need to either sink both of them or leave both of them in the back half of your "COC," you'll naturally feel some pressure. And when you sink both of the remaining putts and achieve your goal, it will instill confidence that you'll take to the course with you when you play your next round.

When you become proficient at leaving putts in the back half of your "COC," it's time to step it up a notch by shrinking the circle to 18 inches. So now the goal becomes to either sink the putt or to leave it in the back half of a circle with a radius of 18 inches around the hole.

Before we move on to chipping and pitching, here are a few more drills you can practice to develop your putting skills.

DISTANCE CONTROL DRILLS

Distance control is important in both "back-half" putts and "lag" putts. Here are two distance control drills. You can practice these drills either on the putting green at your local golf course or at home. And you can practice both "back-half" and "lag" putting.

DISTANCE CONTROL DRILL #1

You can use one of the holes on your putting green or you can just place a coin or some other marker on the green to represent the hole. A marker would probably be better since this drill is about developing distance control – not about sinking putts.

Take a golf club (an alignment rod works too if you use them) and place it 3 feet beyond the hole or the marker. To develop your "back half" putting skill, pick a distance between 5 and 15 feet.

The goal is to stroke the putt past the hole or your marker without hitting the golf club. When you can do this consistently, your putting should improve and your scores should drop because you have developed the distance control skill necessary to get the ball to the hole yet still leave it inside the "circle of confidence" if you miss.

To develop this skill even further, make the drill more challenging by gradually moving the golf club closer to the hole or marker. When the golf club is 18 inches behind the hole and you can still consistently stroke your putts such that they get to the hole and still don't hit the golf club, then you really have your distance control honed in! You'll rarely miss an 18-inch putt, right?

To shift this drill to a "lag" putting drill, just putt from a further distance – 15 feet or further. If you hit the golf club, you've stroked the putt too hard. And if you've left the putt short of the hole or marker, you can eyeball whether or not you've left the putt inside the "circle of confidence."

To really hone in your "lag" putting distance control, slowly reduce the size of your target circle down to 18 inches. When you can consistently "lag" putts into an 18-inch circle, you've really got your distance control dialed in.

You can easily adapt this drill to be practiced at home if you don't have time to go to the course or if it's raining outside. And of course you can simulate the pressure of a real round of golf by setting goals and committing to keep practicing until you reach them.

And if you really want to simulate the pressure, you can force yourself to not only "lag" your first putt inside the "circle of confidence" but also make the second putt. Set a goal to two-putt 5 or 10 times in a row. Or 4 times out of 5 (80% of the time).

And each time you achieve the goal, make it a little harder next time. You'll only keep improving your golf skills if you keep challenging yourself to do a little bit better each time.

You can either set a harder goal or strive to reach the goal more quickly. For example if your goal was to two-putt 5 times in a row and it took you 10 tries to do it, you could either set a goal to two-putt 6 times in a row next time OR you could keep the same goal of two-putting 5 times in a row but try to do it in less than 10 attempts.

DISTANCE CONTROL DRILL #2: THE TOWEL DRILL

This distance control drill is especially for practicing your "back-half" putts. Grab a towel. You could use your golf towel or any other towel. The smaller the towel, the more challenging the drill. You could even use your golf jacket or pullover in a pinch. It simply something to use as a target.

Ideally the towel will be about 36 inches wide and 18 inches deep. That's ideal because it will train you to stroke putts that make it to the hole so you'll sink the putt if you have the correct line. And it will also train to stroke putts with a pace such that the ball comes to rest no more than 18 inches to the left, right, or past the hole leaving you an easy tap-in putt.

Don't be overly concerned with the dimensions of the towel though. Any towel reasonably close to 36" x 18" is fine and your golf towel will probably be just fine. You may even want to find a specific towel for this drill and keep it in your golf bag.

Set the towel on the putting green – or on the carpet if you're practicing at home. Now imagine the front edge of the towel is the hole. Your goal is to stroke the putt such that it comes to a stop on the towel.

Leaving the putt short of the towel is the same as leaving a putt short of the hole on the putting green or on the golf course. Practice this drill to train yourself not to leave "back-half" putts short.

Start from 5 feet or 10 feet, then move out to longer distances as your skill level improves. You'll probably find it's harder than you think.

However, when you can consistently get the ball to stop on the towel, you'll have mastered distance control.

Final Putting Thoughts

If you're going to break 90 on a regular basis, you need to cut your 3-putts down to a minimum. Ideally you would eliminate 3-putts entirely but even the pros 3-putt occasionally so it's not realistic to think you can completely eliminate the 3-putts.

A good goal that will go a long way to breaking 90 consistently is to have no more than 36 putts per round. That averages out to 2 putts per hole. So if you 3-putt once, you can make up for it with a one-putt on another green.

You'd love to one-putt every green or even no-putt when you chip in. And you'll do that on occasion but let's focus on consistently 2-putting every green. That's the critical skill for breaking 90 on a regular basis.

The first step in 2-putting every green is to make your second putt. Obvious, right? And here's how to do it consistently.

Remember, the "circle of confidence" putt I mentioned earlier? That's the type of putt you want for your second putt. That's the type of putt you're going to make most of the time. And if that's the type of putt you leave yourself with, you will 2-putt most greens.

The key is being confident and aggressive from as far away as possible. Everyone is confident they're going to make a one-inch putt or a six-inch putt or even a one-foot putt. Some golfers are still confident and aggressive from 2-feet whereas other golfers start shaking and getting nervous at that distance.

And when you're shaking and nervous standing over a putt, you can forget about making a confident, aggressive stroke. So the key to 2-putting every green (or even 1-putting) is to either:

1) Depending on the type of putt, "lagging" your first putt into your "circle of confidence" OR leaving the putt in the back half of the COC (or just sink the putt!)

OR

2) stick your approach shot (or chip or pitch shot) so close to the pin that you're in confident, aggressive putting mode (and hopefully one-putt)

We've just covered #1 in detail. Practice the drills to develop your putting skills and increase your confidence.

Now let's move on to…

CRITICAL GOLF SKILL #2:
CHIPPING AND PITCHING THE GOLF BALL ON TO THE GREEN (AND NEAR THE HOLE)

It goes without saying that hitting more greens in regulation will lower your score – especially when you 2-putt most greens. And while you should strive to hit more greens in regulation, you're not going to do it every time – especially if breaking 90 is a challenge for you.

Note: "Greens in regulation" (or GIR) is a common golf term that I'll define in case you're not familiar with it. All it means is putting your golf ball on the green in two shots less than par for the particular hole you're playing. If you hit the green in regulation, you ought to 2-putt for par.

So on par 3's, you'll "hit the green in regulation" if you put your tee shot on the putting surface. For par 4's you'll get credit for a GIR if you hit the green with your second shot. And finally for par 5's hitting the green with your third shot (or even your second shot for long-hitters) will result in a GIR.

Given that players striving to break 90 often miss greens in regulation, it's critical that you develop the skill to get the next shot – usually either a chip or a pitch – on to the green. And of course, the closer to the hole the better.

The ultimate goal is to consistently chip or pitch the ball on to the green and then 2-putt at worst. As your skill improves and you're able to get "up and down" you'll turn these three shots into two. And that will really reduce your scores and help you break 90 consistently.

PITCH SHOTS VS. CHIP SHOTS

A chip shot and a pitch shot are not the same. A chip shot has a lower trajectory and more roll. A pitch shot has a higher trajectory and less roll. With the lower trajectory, the chip shot should hit the ground and roll out or "release" towards the hole.

As a general rule, you can figure the chip shot will travel about 1/3 of the distance in the air and the roll out or "release" the other 2/3 of the distance. For example, a 60-foot chip shit will probably go 20 feet in the air and roll out or release another 40 feet.

Of course the actual distance in the air vs "release" depends on the club you use to chip. A lower lofted club – like a 4-iron or hybrid for example – will have more roll out or "release" than a higher lofted club like a wedge. Since a pitch shot is a shot with more height, the ball should land more softly and roll less.

The set up is a bit different too. You'll tend to have more forward shaft lean with a chip shot to promote better contact. Whereas the pitch shot will have less forward shaft lean (or even no forward shaft lean) and a softer grip with less tension to promote a softer landing with less roll.

Every golfer is different so you need to find out what works best for YOU. However, generally speaking you'll get the ball closer to the hole by keeping the ball closer to the ground.

So a chip shot is generally easier than a pitch shot. You can even chip with a putter if you're just off the green on the fringe and better players often do.

DEVELOPING "FEEL" AROUND THE GREENS

Just as with putting, start by developing "feel' around the greens with your chipping and pitching. Start with an easy chip shot where you have a lot of green to work with. That means you have 20 feet or more of green to work with – in other words there is 20 feet or more of green between your ball and the hole.

At first, don't worry about where the ball ends up. You're just trying to develop "feel" around the greens. We'll work on getting the ball close to the hole later.

Some golfers prefer a certain club or clubs (like a pitching wedge and a sand wedge) and they like to adjust their swing to various distances. Other golfers like to use the same swing with different clubs based on the distance. They may use a 7-iron for longer chips, then work their way down to an 8-iron, a 9-iron, and then wedges for shorter chips.

Either way can work and I generally don't believe in "one-size-fits-all" solutions. You need to practice and experiment and see what works best for YOU.

Spend some time experimenting with different clubs. Some golfers even prefer using a hybrid or a 5-wood around the greens and get very good at it.

Experiment with different grips, different grip pressures (a little tighter vs. a little looser), and different clubs until you get comfortable chipping the ball onto the green. And take notice of how far the ball travels as you experiment.

Experiment with different ball positions to see how the ball reacts when it is positioned near your front foot, your back foot, or in the middle of your stance. For chipping, you'll probably find it best to position the ball further back in your stance as it promotes more forward shaft lean and a downward strike on the ball.

As with putting, remember to swing "through" the ball not "at' the ball. And relax. Tension is your enemy in golf.

Don't get to "wristy" or "flippy" with your stroke. You might even experiment with a stroke similar to a putting strike only with a 7-iron, pitching wedge, or other club. If you try this, remember to keep the triangle formed by your shoulders and the club head intact. The only way to break this triangle is by breaking your wrists.

A common cause of mishits is deceleration. That means slowing down – or decelerating – your club head speed as you're about to strike the ball. This is disastrous to your shot. Don't do it!

One of the fundamentals of golf is to ALWAYS accelerate through impact. This applies to putting, pitching, chipping, and the full swing too.

CHIPPING DRILL

After you've developed some "feel" around the greens, you can move on to drills for getting the ball close to the hole. Start with an easy chip shot – something where you've got 20 feet or more of green between you and the hole.

This is generally an easier chip shot because you've got a lot of green to work with. As you have less and less green to work with, the chip shot can become more challenging.

Depending on the situation you may want to switch to a pitch shot when you don't have much green to work with. We'll get into pitching after we cover chipping.

If you've only got a few feet of green to work with then you are what golfers call "short sided." Those chip shots tend to be more challenging because those are the chip shots where golfers will often decelerate because they think they're going to hit the ball to far so they instinctively slow down the club head just before impact.

Typically the result is terrible - maybe a "fat" or "chunked" shot that may only go a few inches leaving with basically the same challenging shot and wasting a precious stroke.

Another common result is a "thin" or "topped" chip shot that rolls through the green and into the rough on the other side of the green. That's why "short sided" chip shots are more challenging.

So start with an easier chip shot where you have a lot green to work with and you can let your chip shot land on the green and "release" or roll out toward the cup.

Quick Note: Later we're going to cover playing "smart" and thinking one shot ahead. This is a good place to insert a quick comment. When you're hitting your approach shot to the green, think about where you'd like to be for your next shot.

The obvious answer is on the green putting. However, golfers that find it challenging to break 90 don't hit many greens in regulation. That being the case, it may be wise to think about hitting your approach shot such that if you happen to miss the green, you'll leave yourself with a simple chip shot – a shot you're confident you can chip on the green and 2-putt at worst. More on this common sense strategy approach later. Just keep this thought in mind.

Ultimately you'd like to reach a level of skill where you can chip your shots into an imaginary 3-foot circle around the hole – your "circle of confidence." And when you can do that consistently, then shrink the circle until you can consistently chip the ball into an imaginary 18-inch circle around the hole.

You'll probably need work your way up to that level of skill though. So if necessary, start with a larger imaginary circle. For arguments sake, let's say you want to get your chip shots into an imaginary 10-foot circle around the hole. This will leave you with a makeable 10-foot putt. And at worst you ought to 2-putt from 10 feet.

So pick a hole and set a goal that challenges you. At the beginning your goal may be to chip 5 of 10 shots into the imaginary 10-foot circle. When you can do that, slowly make the goal more challenging by increasing it to leaving 6, 8, or even all 10 chip shots inside the 10-foot circle.

Setting a goal simulates the pressure of a real round – especially if you have the discipline to keep practicing until you finally achieve the goal.

And when you feel proficient chipping the ball into a 10-foot circle, shrink the circle to 5 feet, then 3 feet, then 18 inches. Practice this drill from various distances around the green and from various lies to really develop your chipping skill.

Of course keep track of your results day after day and week after week from various distances and with various clubs. You'll gain more confidence as you see your results improve and you'll carry this confidence with you to the golf course.

PITCHING BASICS

Pitching is different than chipping. A chip shot should be your first choice because there's less margin for error. However, sometimes you'll find yourself in a situation that calls for a pitch shot.

This would be when you need to pitch the ball over a bunker for example. Or you may need to pitch the ball to an elevated green. Or there may be no green to work with so you need to pitch the ball over an area of rough between your ball and the flag.

The pitch shot has a higher trajectory so you should generally use a club with more loft. Something like a pitching wedge, a gap wedge, a sand wedge, etc.

Just like with putting and chipping, the first step is to develop a "feel" with your pitching. So just pick a spot – preferably a spot with a lot of green to work with – and practice your pitching with different clubs and various swing lengths.

Remember, there's less forward shaft lean with a pitch shot than with a chip shot and you may even want to play the ball a little more forward in your stance to promote a shot with a higher trajectory.

Experiment with different ball positions. For a pitch shot, you may find you get better results with the ball positioned more forward in your stance than for a chip shot.

Experiment with a looser grip too. A looser grip should result in a softer shot that lands and stops quickly. The more tension you have in your grip, the more the ball tends to "release" or roll out.

So experiment with the looser grip and see what happens. You may discover that you need to swing harder than you think with a pitch shot – especially if you're using a loose grip.

Calibrate your distances with different swings. You could think about a clock and think about taking your backswing to "9 o'clock," "10 o'clock," "11 o'clock," "12 o'clock," etc. and see how far the ball goes. You can calibrate your distances like this for your entire short game: putting, pitching, and chipping.

Once you have developed some "feel" with your pitch shots, you can move on to working on pitching the ball on the green. Remember, the first goal of the pitch shot is to get the ball onto the green so you can two-putt.

The mistake many high-handicap golfers make is trying to get cute and get the ball close to the hole. Then they proceed to miss the green, waste a shot, and leave themselves with another chip or pitch shot. And oftentimes, the second chip or pitch shot is more challenging than the first one. Not a good way to lower your score.

So don't try the "hero" shot that's above your skill level – just pitch the ball onto the green, 2-putt, and move on to the next hole. That's how you keep the big numbers off your scorecard and increase your chances of breaking 90.

PITCHING DRILL

Start simple and build your skill over time. Start with the goal of simply pitching the ball on to the green and leaving yourself with a putt. And start with simple pitches where you have a lot of green to work with.

In a relatively short period of time, you ought to develop enough skill to be pitching 10 in a row on to the green. From there, make the drill more challenging by trying to pitch the ball into an imaginary 10-foot circle around the hole.

Start with a goal that's challenging for your skill level. It may be pitching the ball into the 10-foot circle 5 of 10 times. Then slowly increase that to 6 or 8 of 10 inside the 10-foot circle. And shrink the circle to 5-feet, 3-feet, and ultimately 18-inches.

As your pitching skill develops, practice more challenging shots with worse lies and/or less green to work with. Keep track of your results so you can measure your progress and develop confidence as you see your results improve.

CRITICAL GOLF SKILL #3: TURNING 3 SHOTS INTO 2

The "holy grail" for golfers according to the legendary 9-time major champion Gary Player – is turning 3 shots into 2. In other words getting. The "Black Knight" insists that consistently getting "up and down" from around the green will do more to lower your scores than anything else. It may be the best way to shave strokes of your golf score and lower your handicap.

In order to achieve your goal to consistently break 90, your should strive to reach a level of skill where you can confidently chip or pitch the ball on to the green and then 2-putt. That's 3 shots and developing the skill to get "up and up and down" in 3 shots helps keep the big numbers off your scorecard. That alone will go a long way toward helping your break 90.

However, turning 3 shots into 2 is even better. If you can get "up and down" just a couple of times every round, those may be the few critical strokes that lower your score from the low 90s to the high 80s.

And when you can consistently get up and down and turn 3 shots in to 2, you may be breaking 80 – or shooting in the low to mid 80s at worst. Here's a simple drill to help you develop this valuable, stroke-reducing skill…

THE "HOLY GRAIL" DRILL

You can develop this "holy grail" skill by combining all the skills you'll develop by practicing the putting, chipping, and pitching drills I've already shared.

The "holy grail" drill is simple. Pick a spot off the green that requires either a chip or a pitch shot. Set a goal. This is challenging so you may want to start low. Let's just say we want to "turn 3 into 2" 3 out of 10 times or maybe even just once if you're just starting out. Just make the goal challenging for your skill level.

So you'd play 10 chip or pitch shots from the spot you've selected and see how many times you can get "up and down" which turns 3 shots into 2. This is the ultimate skill for a quality golfer and that's why really good players that shoot low scores spend far more time working on improving their short games than they do pounding drivers to see how far they can hit the ball.

Chicks may dig the long ball and developing the skill to smash the ball farther is certainly valuable, yet you'll reduce your scores and break 90 more quickly and consistently when you focus on shaving strokes by chipping and pitching the ball closer to the hole and sinking more putts.

For that reason, you should spend the majority of your practice time on the short game. It simply isn't important how far you hit your drives if you don't have the skills to consistently pitch and chip the ball on to the green and then 2-putt.

When develop your short game skills to this level, all you'll need to do to break 90 is to hit your tee shots 200+ yards and keep them in play. Keeping your tee shots in play is critical – even more important than how far you hit them.

After all, it's hard to shoot low scores when you're constantly hitting your second shots out of the woods or worse re-teeing and hitting your third shot off the tee.

Then you can hit your approach shots somewhere near the green and let your short game take over. And as you develop your iron shot making skills and hit more greens in regulation, your scores will drop even further. You'll probably be breaking 80 when you combine hitting more greens in regulation with solid short game skills.

So lets move on to....

CRITICAL GOLF SKILL #4: CONSISTENTLY HIT YOUR TEE SHOTS 200+ YARDS (AND IN PLAY!)

The saying "drive for show, putt for dough" is definitely true. Yet don't discount the importance of getting off the tee. Even if you have a stellar short game, you won't break 90 without some proficiency off the tee.

And you don't need to be a long bomber to shoot low scores either. If you can consistently hit your tee shots 200 yards or more – and keep them in play! – you stand a great chance of breaking 90 when you can chip, pitch, and putt with a reasonable amount of skill too.

First things first. Sure distance is important and the generally the longer you can hit your tee shots the better because it leaves a shorter approach shot into the greens. However, if you're serious about shooting lower scores, your fist priority should be keeping your tee shots in play – even if it means sacrificing some distance.

That being said, the best club to use off the tee may not be your driver – especially for golfers with higher handicaps. After all, who cares how far you can hit your driver if you hit it into the woods every 3rd or 4th hole? That's 3 or 4 precious shots you've squandered. And possibly many more if you don't play smart golf and get yourself out of trouble – more on playing smart later.

In many cases – especially with golfers who can't consistently break 90 – the best club to use off the tee is a 3-wood, a 5-wood, or even a hybrid club. It's a fact that it's easier to keep these clubs in play because they have more loft which makes them easier to hit straighter.

Some golfers may even prefer to hit a 3-iron or a 4-iron off the tee. That's fine too. If that's the club you can consistently hit 200+ yards AND keep it in play, then that's the club you should use until you develop the skill to hit a hybrid or a wood off the tee.

You can work on your consistency with your woods on the driving range and start using those clubs on the course when you develop enough skill that you can trust them off the tee during a real round of golf.

BOTTOM LINE: Off the tee, use the club you can hit 200+ yards and keep in play most consistently.

You can work towards using longer clubs by practicing on the driving range until eventually you can use your driver on the course and be confident that you can consistently keep it on play. For purposes of the following discussion on the driver swing, I'll assume you're hitting a hybrid club or a wood.

Today's hybrid clubs are so easy to hit that even if you don't yet have the skill to consistently hit your driver or 3-wood and keep it in play, you ought to be able to hit a 3 or 4-hybrid club. However, it's no problem if you're more consistent with a long-iron.

THE DRIVER SWING

Describing the golf swing can be complicated. There's been much written on it and there are often contradictory opinions. As I said, I'm not a professional golf instructor and I don't use much golf jargon.

You see, there are players who are super technical and there are others who learn by "feel." I'm the latter. I don't want somebody to overload me with complex "golfspeak." I just want somebody to show me the proper technique either in person or on video. Or watch me and explain what I need to fix in plain English.

For example, I've heard experts talk about "cupping" the wrists and "bowing" the wrists while showing video. I've seen it dozens if not hundreds of times – and I still don't know what the heck they're talking about!

So I'll leave the complicated swing mechanics and swing thoughts for other people who are more qualified to teach that way and for people who actually want to learn that way, fair enough?

However, if you want to explore the fundamentals of the golf swing in more detail on your own, I highly recommend Ben Hogan's classic book: ***Five Lessons: The Modern Fundamentals of Golf*** (that's the book cover on the right.)

I first read this book about 10 years ago and I've read it several times since. It's the best book I've ever read on the fundamentals of the golf swing written by one of the greatest golfers of all time. It does a better job of describing all the complexities of the golf swing than I could ever dream of doing.

Remember, the ultimate goal of this program is to help you break 90 as quickly as possible – not to make you a scratch golfer. So for all those reasons, I'm only going to cover the basics of the golf swing – enough to get you consistently shooting scores below 90 as quickly as possible. And I'm going to try to keep it as simple as possible.

Let's get started…

Start in a Athletic Position

Before you ever even grip the club, think about putting yourself in a naturally athletic position. You've probably played other sports. Think about a baseball shortstop or centerfielder before the pitch or a football cornerback before the ball is snapped or basketball player in a defensive position.

They are all in a similar relaxed athletic position. They don't stand straight up. Their knees are slightly bent and their upper torso is leaning slightly forward. They're not standing flat-footed. Their weight is more on their toes and their ready to move in any direction as soon as the baseball is hit or the football is snapped.

This is the basic golf stance – and that's what I mean be a relaxed athletic position. Every golfer is a bit different. Some are tall while others are short. Some are skinny and some are stout. So their stances may not be identical but good golfers all start with an athletic stance as I've described with the feet about shoulder width apart and the upper torso leaning slightly forward.

THE BASIC GRIP

Ben Hogan does a great job of describing the grip in excruciating detail. And I'm sure you can find volumes written about the golf grip online so I'm not going to regurgitate it here. Do a simple Internet search on "Ben Hogan golf grip" and you'll get dozens of results including videos.

As I've said and I'm sure I'll repeat again – I don't believe in "one-size-fits-all" solutions and that applies to the golf grip too. Sure there is a basic way to grip the club and it's virtually impossible to play good golf if you violate these fundamentals but there are several variations.

For example, some golfers prefer to interlock the fingers while others prefer to overlap the fingers. You can play good golf either way. What's important is to experiment and find a grip that's comfortable for YOU!

Again though, before moving on, I want to emphasize relaxing. Remember, tension is the enemy of the golf swing. That applies to the grip too. Many golfers – especially those who can't consistently break 90 – grip the golf club with too much tension – too much grip pressure.

The best example I've heard about grip pressure is to think about holding a small bird. You'd want to hold the bird in both hands with enough pressure to prevent the bird from flying way. Yet at the same time you don't want to crush the bird to death either.

Think about that when you're gripping the golf club. Relax your grip. You don't need to hold the club with a "death grip." Here's another thought. Think of holding a breadstick like a golf club. You don't need to hold the breadstick so tightly that you crush it. You can hold it with a relaxed grip that doesn't damage the breadstick.

Make a mental note to experiment with slightly less grip pressure next time you're practicing. This applies to putting, chipping, and pitching as well as to the regular golf swing.

Don't worry about the golf club coming out of your hands. The truth is that if you're swinging the golf club properly, your grip pressure will naturally increase a bit near impact so the club won't fly out of your hands. If that happens you probably need new grips!

It's amazing how much better "feel" you'll develop around the greens and how much farther you'll hit the golf ball when you relax your grip!

Set Up: Addressing the Ball

Set up with a relaxed athletic stance and a relaxed grip on the club. The ball should be positioned forward in your stance because the tee shot is the only shot in golf where you want to hit slightly up on the ball to get it up in the air so it flies farther.

[Note: The exception could be if you hit your tee shots with an iron you may actually want to hit down on the ball.]

The Swing

This is where it can get complex. However, I'm going to do my best to keep it simple. I'll start with an overall way to think about the golf swing and then show the proper position at various points of the golf swing.

The way to practice is to stop your swing at various points and take a look at your hands, your arms, your head, your golf club, etc. and make sure you're in the proper position. If you're not in the proper position, figure out why, and fix it!

It won't be difficult to figure out why you're out of position. It's usually because you're manipulating the club with your hands when you shouldn't be! Just keep practicing putting yourself in the right positions at address, midway through the backswing, at the top of the big swing, when you're firing through to impact, and after impact.

We'll cover the most common swing faults that cause hooks and the dreaded slice soon. I'll explain what causes them and most importantly, I'll provide simple solutions to cure you of these golf ailments.

Before we get to that though, let's cover some basic fundamentals about how to properly swing a golf club and hit the golf ball with power – and to be able to repeat this powerful swing over and over again.

"Hammer" the Ball!!!

This isn't going to be some complicated explanation about the laws of science and how they relate to the golf swing. It's just a simple analogy that should help you see the big picture and help you make some sense out of the golf swing.

And when you understand the theory the behind how to strike the golf ball properly it follows that you'll have more success, right?

The best analogy I've ever heard about striking a golf ball is that it's similar to a hammer hitting a nail. And it makes a lot of sense when you think about it because both involve the control of a swinging implement.

In this analogy, the hammer is like the golf club and the nail is like the golf ball. The head of the hammer is like the head of the golf club. The faster the head of the hammer is moving through impact the more powerfully you'll strike the nail and the deeper you'll drive it into the wood.

Similarly, the faster the head of the golf club is moving at impact the more powerfully you'll strike the ball and the deeper you'll drive it into the fairway!

Think about how you grip the hammer. It's a relaxed grip not a "death grip." This is because a "death grip" would add tension and restrict the free flowing movement of the wrist – and that would restrict the speed of the hammer's head and result in a less powerful swing.

The swing of the hammer is initiated by the small muscles of the hand and wrist, however once in motion the weight of the hammer's head takes over.

On the backswing, you don't consciously cock your wrist. The wrist naturally hinges or cocks as the weight of the hammer moves toward the top of the backswing. There may be a slight pause at the top, but once the transition into the downswing is initiated the weight of the hammer's head naturally takes over again.

You don't physically maneuver the hammer with your hands and wrists. Doing so would actually hinder the downswing, reducing the speed of the hammer and thus the power with which it smashes the nail.

The wrist really just acts as a lever that allow the head of the hammer to reach its maximum speed. And finally, you don't hit "at" the nail, you swing "through" the nail. You literally are trying to drive the nail through the wood.

That's a great analogy to swinging a golf club. On the back swing, there's absolutely no need to cock your wrists. And in fact, consciously cocking your wrists is actually detrimental to achieving maximum club head speed and delivering a powerful blow on the golf ball through impact.

Similar to how the weight of the hammer's head will naturally cock your wrist when you swing a hammer, let the weight of the club head naturally cock your wrists on the back swing.

Then when you reach the top of the backswing, don't use the small muscles of the hands and wrists, let the big muscles of the shoulders, back, and your core initiate the transition from the backswing to the downswing.

Again, the weight of the club head will naturally uncock or unhinge your wrists. There's no need at all for you to consciously manipulate the club with your wrists, let the weight of the club head do it naturally – and more powerfully!

Manipulating the club head by consciously uncocking your wrists leads to what's referred to as "casting." Casting is a great way to zap the power out of your golf swing because you'll reach maximum club head speed before you hit the ball!

By the time your club head reaches the ball the power is gone and the ball won't fly as far. When you eliminate "casting," you'll add "lag" to your swing. And that's great because more "lag" means more club head speed. And more club head speed adds distance to your golf shots.

I'll share a drill you can use to see if you're "casting" your golf club. And you can use the same drill to eliminate casting and add power to your golf swing. The final point of the "hammer-nail" to "golf club-golf ball" analogy is this…

You've probably hammered so many nails into boards that you don't really think about what you're doing anymore. You just grab the hammer and pound the nail through the wood. You've done it so much that it's become natural and instinctive.

When you strike a nail with a hammer, you're not hitting "at" the nail, you're accelerating "through" the nail literally trying to drive the nail through the wood. That's a perfect analogy to the correct approach for striking a golf ball with a golf club.

You don't want to hit "at" the golf ball. You'll get much better results if you accelerate through impact. A swing thought I've found helpful is to swing "through" the ball not "at" the ball.

With practice, swinging a golf club will become as natural and instinctive as swinging a hammer. And with proper practice, you can reach this point relatively quickly. You'll just "grip it and rip it" without thinking about it.

There's no need to clog your head with a bunch of confusing swing thoughts. I've come to think that confusing us may be part of the golf industry's strategy. They throw so much complicated theory at us and fill our heads with so many little things we need to think about that we're overloaded with information and we're not sure what the heck to do.

So we keep buying more golf magazines, swing aids, and expensive lessons! Trust me, golf does not need to be that complicated. We'll cover the golf swing and a few simple positions you should be in at various points along the swing as well as some practice drills in a minute.

Swing the SledgeHammer

A similar but slightly different way to picture the golf swing might to think about swinging a sledgehammer. It takes two hands to swing a sledgehammer. Think about how you would swing the sledgehammer to demolish a piece of drywall by hitting the wall at the bottom such that you would be swinging the sledgehammer similar to how you would swing a golf club.

A sledgehammer is much heavier that a golf club so it's harder to manipulate with the small muscles of the hands. Instead you just get the sledgehammer started in the right direction and let the weight of the sledgehammer take over.

You smash the head of the sledgehammer through the drywall. That's the same idea to have when you're hitting a golf ball with a golf club. A golf club is much lighter than a sledgehammer yet you should resist the natural temptation to manipulate the golf club with your hands and let the weight of the golf club do the work just like the weight of the sledgehammer does.

You don't want to hit "at" the golf ball. You'll get much better results if you accelerate through impact. A swing thought I've found helpful is to swing "through" the ball not "at" the ball.

Trying swinging the golf club as if it's a sledgehammer and your knocking out some drywall. "Hammer" the club head through the ball not "at" the ball.

With practice, swinging a golf club will become as natural and instinctive as swinging a hammer or a sledgehammer. And with proper practice, you can reach this point relatively quickly. You'll just "grip it and rip it" without thinking about it.

There's no need to clog your head with a bunch of confusing swing thoughts. I've come to think that confusing us may be part of the golf industry's strategy. They throw so much complicated theory at us and fill our heads with so many little things we need to think about that we're overloaded with information and we're not sure what the heck to do.

So we keep buying more golf magazines, swing aids, and expensive lessons! Trust me, golf does not need to be that complicated. We'll cover the golf swing and a few simple positions you should be in at various points along the swing as well as some practice drills in a minute.

However, before we do that I want to share a few more basic fundamentals of the golf swing – specifically an important source of power.

Like Shooting a Rubber Band…

Now you understand why swinging a golf club is like swinging a hammer. Another key to developing a powerful, repeatable golf swing is found in an analogy to shooting rubber bands.

Most of us used to shoot rubber bands when we were in school. We'd shoot them across the room trying to hit our friends – or even our teachers. The same tension that allowed us to shoot the rubber band farther can help us hit the golf ball farther.

Tension is generally the enemy of the golf swing. This is the exception. This type of tension allows you to put a powerful swing on the golf ball and pound it farther.

Think about shooting a rubber band. You hold it in one finger – or maybe a thumb – and pull it back as far as you can. The farther back you can pull the rubber band, the more tension you create, and the farther the rubber band will fly.

You can create this same type of power producing tension in your golf swing. You do it by creating tension between the upper half of your body and the lower half of your body.

The key producing tension with the rubber band is pulling one end of the rubber band back while holding the other end still – in a constant position. If you were to move your finger back as you pulled the rubber band back, no tension would be created.

In the golf swing, the tension is created between the upper body and the lower body. If you're swinging with correct form you'll feel this tension in your lower back just above the waist. If you don't feel any tension there, then you're losing an important source of power.

Just as the key to creating tension is keeping one point still or "quiet" as you pull the rubber band back, the key to creating power-producing tension in your golf swing is to keep the bottom half of your body still or "quiet" as the top half rotates backwards on the back swing. In golf jargon, keeping the bottom half of your body still is referred to as having a "quiet bottom."

This may sound complicated but that's only because it's challenging to describe in words. It's actually very simple. Here's how to create the power-producing tension between your upper and lower body...

You just keep the bottom half of your body still during the backswing. It's as simple as that. If you have a "quiet bottom" you will fell the tension in your lower back. If you don't feel the tension in your lower back then you are probably rotating your lower body during the backswing as opposed to keeping it still or "quiet."

To test yourself, just keep track of your belt buckle or belly button. They should be basically pointing towards the ball at address. And that's also where they should be pointing at the top of your back swing because your bottom has stayed still or "quiet."

If your belt buckle and belly button have rotated along with your upper body during the backswing then they'll both be pointing backwards at the top of your backswing. This means you don't have a "quiet bottom," you're not creating this important power-producing tension, and your golf swing is lacking a critical source of power.

When you first try to keep your bottom "quiet," it may feel awkward. It requires some strength and flexibility in your core. However, you can work on developing this strength and flexibility while you watch TV or even at the office with a simple drill.

THE "QUIET BOTTOM" DRILL

You don't even need a golf club for this drill. You can do it just about anywhere. Simply take your normal athletic golf stance, then take your back swing with the focus on keeping your bottom half still.

Try keeping your front foot flat on the ground. Lifting your front foot off the ground makes it easier to move your bottom half. Keeping it flat on the ground promotes a "quiet" bottom.

Rotate your upper body as far back as possible to really create the maximum amount of torque and tension. And then go even a little further back to create even more tension!

Doing this drill for just 5 minutes every day will develop strength and flexibility in your core that will help your create the power-producing tension you need for a powerful golf swing.

It would be easy to add 100 more pages to confuse the heck out of you but I'm not going to do it. That's enough for now. If you truly understand and internalize what I've just shared in the last few pages and most importantly incorporate it into your golf swing, you're well on your way to developing a golf swing that's plenty powerful enough to consistently break 90!

Final Swing Thoughts

Relax! Remember the type of tension that restricts the free-flowing naturally movement of the body reduces club head speed and produces a golf swing that's less powerful than it could or should be.

Use the big muscles of the shoulders, back, and core – NOT the little muscles of the hands and wrists. Let the weight of the club head naturally hinge the wrists and produce golf swing as powerful as a hammer pounding a nail.

You could practice this with an "air swing." Just take your swing pretending the club is in your hands. You see professional golfers taking "air swings" on television all the time. They're trying to get the proper "feel" of the golf swing.

The next step is to repeat this swing while actually holding the golf club. Take some practice swings but pretend you aren't holding the club – even though you actually are. This will really show you how the weight of the golf club will naturally hinge your wrists.

Then start hitting golf balls with that same swing. This promotes a golf swing that swings "through" the ball not "at" the ball. Said another way: take your practice swing and let the ball get in the way. Just pretend the ball isn't even there. This will remove the power-killing tension and produce a more powerful strike on the ball that adds distance to every club in your bag.

It can be a challenge to overcome your mind's resistance to this idea. That's why it's so important to understand and internalize the basic fundamentals of the golf swing.

The mind is a powerful thing and if the mind is not on board with the body as to the proper way to swing the golf club, the mind often overpowers the body and sabotages the golf swing.

OK, enough on the basic fundamentals of the golf swing. Here's how to put all this into practice so you can break 90 soon.

A SIMPLE DRILL FOR HITTING 200+ YARD DRIVES ... AND KEEPING THEM IN PLAY TOO!

Golfing great Nick Faldo uses this drill. I've seen him demonstrate it. And if it's good enough for Sir Nick – a 6-time major champion – then it's good enough for you and me!

Before we get started, I'll remind you that the goal is hit the ball 200+ yards off the tee AND keep it in play too!! Keeping it in play is critical. What good does it do to smash your drives 250 yards, 275 yards, 300 yards or more if you don't have second shot much of the time!

If that's the case, you're throwing precious shots away. And perhaps even more damaging is the fact that you're putting yourself in bad positions. Instead of just getting yourself out of trouble, the tendency – especially for testosterone-filled males! – is to try some kind of "hero" shot.

That's a great way to increase your scores because more often than not, you don't pull off the "hero" shot and leave yourself in an even worse position. That's when you put the big numbers on the card – the 7's, 8's, 9's, and even 10+'s – that destroy your chances of breaking 90.

A huge part of breaking 90 is playing smart golf. That means when you get into trouble, you take your medicine and get out of trouble! That means you play smart golf off the tee and keep yourself out of trouble to begin with!

And that means using the club the gives you the best chance of hitting the ball 200+ yards AND keeping it in play. If that club is not the driver, so what? Do you want to shoot low scores or do you want to smash your drives 300 yards and into the woods half the time?

If you're more concerned with distance than with shooting low scores, there's nothing wrong with that. That probably makes you like most golfers.

However, if that's the case, this program is not for you! This is for golfers serious about developing the golf skills necessary to consistently break 90. End of sermon!

This applies to the 14 par 4 and par 5 holes you'll play on most courses. And instead of teeing the ball up and wildly swinging as hard as possible, we'll take the opposite approach. You'll start with shorter swings and gradually lengthen your swing as you develop more control and accuracy.

Pull out your driver, place a ball on a tee, and start small. Try to "chip" the ball out 75 yards. Pick a target. If you're at the driving range, there should be a marker or a flag you can shoot at.

"Chip" 8 to 10 drives out to 75 yards. When you become proficient at that distance, raise the bar and "chip" your drive out to 100 yards. Do it until you can consistently "chip" your drive out to the 100-yard marker.

If you can't do it with your driver, no problem – move down to a 3-wood, a 5-wood, a hybrid, or even a long iron – a 3-iron or 4-iron – whatever club you're most confident hitting.

Once you've found your "driver" keep increasing the distances. Move on to a target 150 yards out, then 200 yards. As you increase the target distance your swing will naturally become longer.

Practice the "chip" drill until you find the club you can consistently hit 200+ yards AND more importantly keep it in play. Sure, all things being equal it's better to hit the fairways. However, for the purposes of breaking 90, just focus on keeping the ball in play so that you have a clear second shot to the green.

If you can't consistently break 90 you shouldn't be playing courses with "US Open" type rough so it really shouldn't matter much if you miss the fairway. It's more important to keep the ball in play.

You can focus on hitting fairways when you're consistently breaking 90 and want to improve even more so you can start breaking 80. Improving your golf game and lowering your scores is a matter of incremental improvements over time.

So let's focus on developing the critical golf skill that allows you consistently hit your drives 200+ yards AND keep them in play for now. Once you reach that minimum skill level, then you can focus on hitting the ball farther and straighter. Fair enough?

If you have a natural draw (the ball drifts slightly left for a right-handed golfer) or a natural fade (the ball drifts slight right for a right-handed golfer), then play it. This can actually be a good thing because it effectively doubles the size of the fairway.

For example, if you have a natural draw and you trust that your shot will naturally drift back the to left, then you can aim down the right hand side of the fairway and "work" the ball back toward the center of the fairway. It would be the opposite if you have a natural fade.

This effectively doubles the size of the fairway as opposed to the golfer who aims down the middle and only has half the width of the fairway to work with to the left and to the right.

Play your natural shot shape to your advantage. Of course, there are techniques for hitting a draw and a fade so you can "work" the ball to the right or to the left. However, those are beyond the scope of this program.

Our focus is simple. We want you to develop the critical golf skills necessary to consistently break 90 as quickly as possible. And one of those critical skills is getting off the tee successfully with a drive that is consistently both 200+ yards in length AND consistently in play.

We don't need to overcomplicate things by trying to "work" the ball left and right. We'll save that for when you're successfully breaking 90 with ease and your focus turns to breaking 80. Fair enough?

When you find the club that you can consistently hit 200+ yards and within the bounds of what you know to be a typical fairway width, then congratulations! You've developed a golf skill critical to breaking 90.

However, don't be satisfied with hitting your drives 200 yards off the tee and keeping them in play. Keep practicing. When you've found the club you can consistently hit 200 yards and at least near the fairway, keep pushing the envelope. Strive for 225 yards, 250 yards, and more.

And if you're hitting less than a real driver off the tee, work your way up to hitting the driver. The driver can be a challenging club to hit. And frankly there's no crime in hitting 3-wood off the tee – especially on more narrow holes that require more precise tee shots.

I recall Henrik Stenson recently winning the FedEx Cup and the $10 million that comes with it by mainly hitting 3-wood off the tee. If a touring PGA pro can win $10 million hitting 3-wood off the tee, there's certainly nothing wrong with you hitting 3-wood off the tee. If that's the club that gives you the best chance of shooting low scores, then by all means use it!

So there you have it. There's your simple drill. It may sound a bit strange to be "chipping" your drives yet I'm confident you'll make some amazing discoveries about this wonderful game called golf.

First by focusing on a smooth swing that produces a shot of say 150 or 175 yards as opposed to a wild, flailing swing to hit the ball to Mars, I believe you'll be amazed at how far you hit the ball.

This is because with a more controlled swing you'll be hitting the ball more solidly and more near the "sweet spot" center of the club. You'll probably be amazed when you see you're actually hitting the ball just as far as you do with your normal driver swing.

And secondly, this drill promotes a more smooth and controlled swing as opposed to the wild, flailing "swing for the fences" swing that produces inconsistent results for so many golfers who can't consistently break 90.

This drill also promotes a more relaxed, free-flowing swing that eliminates distance destroying tension.

So there you have it. A simple drill for getting off the tee and developing the skill and confidence to break 90 not just occasionally but every time you tee it up!

If you're still finding it challenging to develop this critical golf skill, don't worry. You're not alone. Golf is a very challenging game. Here are some simple cures to the most common challenges for playing better golf and consistently breaking 90.

COMMON FAULTS AND FIXES

COMMON FAULT #1: POWER ZAPPER #1 – THE REVERSE PIVOT

If you're swinging with a "reverse pivot" pay close attention because you can quickly add 50 to 100 yards to your drives with one simple fix.

So what is a "reverse pivot?" In simple terms, golfers with a "reverse pivot" have their weight moving away from the target. For maximum power, you want your weight moving towards the target at impact.

It's a simple fact of sports (and probably physics too!). Think about a baseball pitcher, a football quarterback, or a tennis player serving the ball. What do they have in common?

They all have their weight moving forward to produce maximum power. The baseball pitcher is stepping towards home plate as he releases the pitch. Can you imagine how weak the pitch would be if his weight was moving backwards – away from home plate?

And the best hitters are stepping into the pitch as they swing the bat too. They're not falling backwards.

The football quarterback is stepping forward as he launches the long bomb downfield. Do you really think Peyton Manning could heave the football 50 or 60 yards down the field with a "reverse pivot" that had his weight moving backwards as he threw the pass? Not likely.

And the tennis player with the 100+ mph serve also has his weight moving forward toward his opponent as he smashes the ball. There are probably a dozen more examples but I'm certain you get the point…

To produce maximum power in your golf swing, you need to have your weight moving forward! Yet for some reason many golfers have their weight moving backwards at impact.

This is a very common fault for high handicap golfers who can't consistently break 90. Fortunately there's a quick and simple fix that could add 50 to 100 yards or more to your drives almost instantly!

THE FIX: "HAPPY GILMORE" DRILL

Remember the movie "Happy Gilmore"? Not quite as good as Caddyshack in my humble opinion but still a classic golf movie. You'll recall Adam Sandler took his hockey swing to the golf course.

He actually ran towards his tee shots and annihilated them! It was a fictional movie of course yet the principal is no fantasy. It's a fact that when you throw your weight towards the target in any sport you'll add power.

In golf, it couldn't be more simple. Gary Player was famous for stepping into his shots. And you can add power to your golf game by taking a page out of The Black Knight's playbook.

You can develop this weigh transfer skill by stepping into your shots. How you choose to do it isn't so important but here's how to insure your weight is moving forward at impact.

End your swing on your front foot. Your weight cannot possibly be going backwards if you end your swing on your front foot or you will fall straight down on your arse!

Perhaps the simplest way to do this is to actually take a step after you hit the ball. You can do this by shifting your weight to your front foot (the left foot for a right-handed golfer), then taking a step forward with your other foot (the right foot for a right-handed golfer).

It may be awkward at first and it may look funny, yet it promotes the forward weight shift that eliminates one the most common power zappers for high-handicap golfers – the "reverse pivot."

COMMON FAULT #2: THE SLICER'S DELIGHT – OVER THE TOP

If you're slicing your drives, there's a good chance your swing path is "over the top." Or in plain English, you cut across the ball with a swing path that goes from outside to inside – outside the ball to inside the ball.

This puts a vicious right to left sidespin on the ball that makes it fly to the right – for a right-handed golfer. It would be the opposite for a left-handed golfer.

The shot will typically start to the left or down the middle until it takes a hard right. That's because the initial strike on the ball is powerful enough to overcome the slice spin. However, eventually the spin takes over and that's when the ball takes a hard right-hand turn.

While an "over the top" swing path normally produces a slice, it can sometimes produce a shot that's pulled way left. That's because occasionally you may strike the ball squarely enough that you don't impart much of the slice producing right to left sidespin on the ball.

However, since your swing path is going from outside to inside – cutting across the ball from right to left if you were standing behind a right-handed golfer, your shots will head straight left absent the sidespin.

If this describes your shots, here's the cure for your ails...

THE FIX: "OTT BLOCKER" DRILL

The simple solution is similar to how I avoid eating "junk food." I don't go to fast food restaurants and I don't buy crap like potato chips and TV dinners at the grocery store.

That being the case, these "junk foods" are never around to entice me. And by eliminating the availability of these crap foods, I eliminate the temptation to eat them. You can use the same principle to eliminate your slice. Here's how...

You simply eliminate the option of swinging the golf club with an "over the top" outside to inside swing path. It's easy to do.

Next time you're at the driving range, set up your ball on a tee like you would for a normal drive. Then before you hit a shot, place an obstacle in the way that prevents you from swinging "over the top."

For a right-handed golfer, this means placing something behind and just to the right of the golf ball. It could be a tee you stick in the ground, it could be another golf ball, it could be a club head cover, or it could be something else. It just needs to be an obstruction that prevents you from making solid contact with the ball if you make an "over the top" swing path. Now hit your tee shot!

With that impediment in the way, it's not possible to hit the ball solidly with an improper swing path. If you swing with an "over the top" swing path you'll hit whatever you've placed in the way before you hit the ball.

This will probably feel very awkward at first – especially if you're a life long slicer. Be patient, keep practicing, give it some time and eventually you'll eliminate your "over the top" swing path and your slice.

If you're not careful, you might just find yourself hitting a slight draw that increases your distance off the tee!

COMMON FAULT #3: THE "QUICK" HOOKER – FORE LEFT!!!

First the good news. If your golf shots are consistently taking a hard left (or a hard right if you're a left-handed golfer), you're probably closer to breaking 90 than you think.

It's easier to go from "hooking" the ball to playing good golf than it is to go from "slicing" the ball and playing good golf. It's a natural progression. Golfers tend to start with a "reverse pivot" and an "over the top" swing path, then over correct to hooking their shots.

So if you've started with hooking the ball – in other words your shots tend to take a hard left OR a hard right if you're a left-handed golfer – then you're actually ahead of the game. Congratulations! You ought to be breaking 90 in no time once we fix your hook.

There are two common causes to being a "hooker". You probably either have swing that's just too darn quick OR you have an "inside to outside" swing path that puts a left to right sidespin on the ball. Either challenge is easily fixable.

"HOOKER" FIX #1: THE SLOW MOTION DRILL (SLOW DOWN)

If you're swing is too quick, just slow it down. Easier said than done of course, however you've probably fallen victim to the natural inclination – especially if you have a male appendage between your legs – to over swing. You just swing too darn hard and fast.

Just to be crystal clear, I'm not talking about club head speed. You can swing 130 mph or more and you'll be fine as long as you have proper form. Yet most golfers that try to increase their club head with a swing they perceive to be faster in their minds are actually destroying their swing with other common errors.

Here's the problem with a swing that's too quick: When you speed up your swing, your hands naturally tend to close the club face before impact. And any golfer worth his or her salt understands hitting the ball with a closed club face imparts "hook" spin on the ball.

Simply slow down the swing and you're more likely to strike the ball with a square club face and hit the ball straight. Use the "chip" drill I described earlier. Not only will this drill slow down your swing, it will also probably have you striking the ball more squarely which adds distance.

"HOOKER" FIX #2: THE "ITO" BLOCKER DRILL

Another cause of the "hooks" is an inside-to-outside swing path. This is the opposite of the outside-to-in swing path I described earlier. An inside-to-outside swing path imparts a left to right sidespin on the ball.

Initially the shot may start out down the middle and stay there for a while until it eventually takes a hard left (or a hard right for a left-handed golfer) as the force of the initial strike gives way to the sidespin.

The cure to this is simple – eliminate the possibility of striking the ball with an inside-to-outside swing path. Place an obstruction in the way such that it's not possible to strike the ball cleanly without hitting the tee, the ball, the club head cover, or whatever else you've placed in the way to prevent an inside-to-outside swing path.

Again, it will probably feel very awkward at first because the obstruction prevents you from taking what has become your natural swing. However, the more you practice, the more comfortable as you'll get and the straighter you'll hit the ball.

COMMON FAULT #4: PLAYING BASEBALL (LINE DRIVES AND GROUND BALLS)

This is one of the most common golf ailments and the one with the simplest solution. If you're not hitting majestic tee shots and flag seeking approach shoots with pinpoint accuracy, there could be countless causes…

However, if the problem that plagues you is hitting low line drives or even worse ground balls like a baseball player in a terrible slump, that narrows down what may be the root cause of your bad golf shots. It all boils down to natural human tendencies and there's a simple solution.

You've probably fallen victim to natural human inclination towards curiosity. More specifically you're curious about where your shot is headed. The problem – and it's a HUGE problem – is that you're probably taking a peek **before** you actually make contact with the golf ball.

And since everything is connected you're "topping the ball." When you peek or take a look before you make contact with the ball it sets in motion a chain reaction that is disastrous to any golfer with hopes of making clean, crisp contact with the golf ball.

When you take a peek, your entire head tends to rise even if it's only incrementally. And since your shoulders are closely connected to your head, your shoulders rise up a bit.

Unfortunately that's not the end of this "bad golf "chain reaction – only the beginning. Your arms and hands are connected to your shoulders so they rise as well – even if it's only an inch or two.

You can probably see where this is headed. Your hands are connected to your arms and you're holding the golf club in your hands. And considering how small a golf ball is there's a small margin for error when it comes to making solid contact.

Here's the bottom line: If you peek just a fraction of a second before impact – and the majority of golfers who can't consistently break 90 have a tendency to peek! – you've practically eliminated your chances of making clean, crisp contact.

Considering you're moving everything up – even if it's just a fraction of an inch – it's common sense that you'll tend to "top" the golf ball. Chances are you'll hit it just a bit above the top of center and that's all it takes to "skull" the ball which results in a low line drive or even a ground ball.

THE FIX: THE 1,001 DRILL

The solution is both obvious and simple. Don't peek!! Suppress the natural human urge to want to see the result of the golf shot before you actually hit the golf shot.

While in theory that's easy to say, in practice it's extremely difficult for many golfers to put into practice due to their natural human inclination to be curious and to take a peek before they ever make contact with the golf ball.

This can be an especially challenging tendency to overcome when you're just starting out and your ball striking is inconsistent. You'll probably be spraying the ball all over the place and feel like you need to peek to see where the heck the ball is headed. I know this from personal experience.

Yet as I practiced the drills I'm sharing with you and my ball striking improved I hit the ball more consistently and more straight which instilled more confidence in where the ball was going and reduced the need to take a peek at where the shot was headed.

It can be a difficult bridge to gap. Yet you must do it if you want to improve your ball striking. Start at the driving range – not at the course. Take your regular swing and as challenging as it may be force yourself to first strike the golf ball and then – only after you've struck the golf ball – to wait one second before you lift your head to follow the shot.

It's like this. Strike the ball. Count "one thousand and one." And then – and only then – can you even attempt to follow the ball with your eyes. Over time, as you become a better driver of the ball and a better striker of the golf ball with your irons, you'll become more consistent and you won't need to peek.

You'll naturally know how far you hit the ball and you'll know where to look after waiting a second to look for the ball. Believe me, I know it's easier said than done. Yet if you want to play better golf and shoot scores in the 90's you absolutely must stop peeking before you actually strike the ball.

Eliminating mis-hits – and that includes "fat" shots as well as the "thin" line drive and ground ball shots we're talking about here – goes an incredibly long way to shaving off strokes and consistently breaking 90.

Stop peeking and it's likely you'll stop hitting "thin" shots. We'll cover eliminating "fat" shots a bit later. Now let's move on to…

COMMON FAULT #5: CASTING (POWER ZAPPER #2)

I referred to "casting" earlier. It's a big power zapper because when you "cast" the golf club your club head reaches maximum speed before impact. And by the time the golf club actually makes impact with the golf ball, club head speed is reduced resulting in a less powerful strike robbing you of distance.

The root cause of "casting" is using your hands and wrists at the beginning of the downswing. The weight of the club will naturally unhinge your wrists so there's no need to even think about it – just let it happen naturally. Remember, the golf swing is similar to swinging a hammer.

So are you "casting" the golf club? Here's a simple drill that will both help you determine if you are "casting" and provide feedback to fix the problem.

THE FIX: THE "WHOOSH" DRILL

The "whoosh" drill works best with an alignment rod but you can use a golf club too. All you do is take your normal full-speed swing and listen for the "whoosh" the rod or the club makes as it cuts through the air.

You'll hear the "whoosh" at the point in your swing where you reach maximum club head speed. That being the case, if you're swinging the golf club properly you should hear the "whoosh" at the bottom of your swing where you make impact with the golf ball.

If you're "casting," however, you will hear the "whoosh" well before you reach the impact position. You'll hear the "whoosh" during the down swing well before you reach the impact position.

Again, the cause is that you're consciously uncocking or unhinging your wrists on the down swing instead of allowing the weight of the club head to do it naturally.

It will probably feel a bit awkward at first but you must learn to allow the big muscles of the shoulders, back, and core do most of the work. The little muscles of the hands and wrists just follow naturally.

Try taking practice swings without a golf club. Then grip a golf club and take practice swings pretending you aren't even holding a golf club even though you are. When you do this, you'll notice how the weight of the club head will naturally hinge and unhinge your wrists.

There's no need to consciously manipulate the club with the little muscles of the hands and wrists. And in fact doing so is detrimental to the golf swing. Let it happen naturally – just like you would while swinging a hammer.

When you're got it down, you'll hear the "whoosh" at the impact position, you'll create powerful "lag" that increases club head speed, and you'll notice how much farther you're hitting the golf ball too!

OK then, let's move on the next critical golf skill…

CRITICAL GOLF SKILL #5: CONSISTENTLY HIT APPROACH SHOTS NEAR THE GREEN (ON THE GREEN IS EVEN BETTER)

Hitting your approach shots is the link between getting off the tee and taking advantage of the chipping, pitching, and putting skills of your short game. And while hitting more greens should certainly lower your score and it's an important part of breaking 80, personally I think this is the least important skill for breaking 90.

I say this from personal experience because while I strike my irons much better these days, when I first started consistently breaking 90 several years ago, my iron shots were ugly – and that may be putting it mildly.

Far from the majestic high flying, soft landing shots you see on television or from single-digit handicap golfers, my iron shots had a low ball flight with a strong draw. And while I did not hit many greens in regulation, I was able to advance the ball somewhere near the green.

My iron game was the weak link. However, I was good off the tee and my short game was good enough that if could just "slap" my approach shot up somewhere near the green, I was confident I could at least bogey the hole by pitching or chipping the ball on to the green and 2-putting. And occasionally I would even get up and down for par.

Striking iron shots – especially mid and long irons – can be the biggest challenge for golfers who can't consistently break 90. It certainly was the biggest challenge for me to overcome.

I believe this is because most high-handicap golfers don't understand how to hit crisp iron shots. Specifically they don't understand that to hit the golf ball up in the air with an iron you actually need to strike down on the ball.

It's counterintuitive and it can be difficult to understand because it seems to go against common sense. And even if you do understand the concept of striking down on the golf ball in theory, it can still be difficult to execute the shot.

The biggest problem is that many high-handicap golfers have the mistaken belief that they need to swing under the ball or "scoop" the ball in order to get it air born. However, you'll never hit sold iron shots trying to strike the golf ball like this.

Trying to "scoop" the ball up into the air is a major cause of both "fat" shots that go nowhere. And "thin" or "topped" shots that tend to be either ground balls or low line drives.

The "fat" shot – also called a "chunk" – happens when you strike the ground behind the ball before actually hitting the ball. This is disastrous because it dramatically reduces club head speed – or it could even completely stop the golf club if you hit far enough behind the ball.

The result is a weak shot that flies considerably less distance than it should or you may even bounce the golf club off the ground and hit a ground ball. Either way it's not good.

Failing to strike down on the golf ball is also the cause of "thin" or "topped" shots that end up as either "worm burners" or low screaming line drives that sail over greens.

These "mis-hits" are very frustrating – I know this from personal experience because I used to hit so many of them! And they can really add up and ruin your score too.

Of course if you're trying to break 80, you'll want to be hitting more greens in regulation. However, remember the main objective of this program is to get you consistently breaking 90 as soon as possible so we have a slightly different goal.

You absolutely want to be working toward hitting more greens in regulations. However, eliminating the "mis-hit" shots with your irons – the "fat" shots, the "chunk" shots, the "thin" shots, the "topped" shots, the "worm burners," the screaming line drives – is the goal for now.

These bad shots are not only detrimental to your state of mind on the course, they also commonly leave you in terrible positions that add even more strokes to your score and more stress to your round.

When you can eliminate these costly mistakes, you may be amazed at how quickly your scores drop. And the solution is so simple: STRIKE THE GOLF BALL BEFORE YOUR CLUB HITS THE GROUND!

Sure it's simple, yet I know from personal experience how challenging it can be to take this simple thought and put it into practice. It just doesn't make logical sense to many golfers that you must hit down on the ball to hit crisp iron shots.

And even if you do understand this critical concept, the mind is often stronger than the body. It was a challenge for me to develop this skill even after I accepted the "hit down on the ball" concept because as I was swinging my brain would take over.

And just before impact, my mind would overrule my brain and I'd end up trying to "scoop" for "flip" the ball up in the air. The result was absolutely horrible iron play for longer than I care to admit!

Bottom Line: To improve your iron game you absolutely must hit the ball before you hit the ground. That's why good golfers leave a divot in front of the ball.

Here's how I finally solved this problem and started hitting better iron shots.

As I often do, I made friends with a low-handicap golfer. This one is a 1-handicap and has been the champion of a golf league I used to play in on several occasions. This is the type of guy you want to study and seek advice from.

One day after our round, I wanted to go to the practice range and hit some balls so I offered to buy him a bucket of balls – yes a bribe! And a cheap golf lesson too!

Specifically, I sought advice on how to improve my poor iron play. His simple advice helped me immensely so I'll pass it on to you. And I'll also share some simple drills to help you ingrain this valuable golf skill – consistently striking the "little ball" (the golf ball) before striking the "big ball" (Earth!).

His simple golf-life changing advice – which took a total of about 30 seconds to dispense – was this: focus on a spot about an inch in front of the ball and hit that spot. Don't focus on hitting the ball; focus on hitting that spot in front of the ball.

Admittedly it's difficult to internalize – especially if you hold on to the mistaken belief that you need to help the ball into the air by "scooping" it. However, I guarantee if you'll just cast your doubts aside and do it, this could be the breakthrough that transforms your golf game to a higher level

– maybe even several levels higher! It's that BIG.

If you need to put a twist on this simple concept, here are a few things I've done. Try putting an object in front of the ball and focus on hitting the object – not an object that obstructs your swing – just a small object.

I've used a ball marker and a penny for example. I don't know about you but improving my poor iron play was well worth the few pennies I lost. You could even use a tee just plant it far enough into the ground that it doesn't obstruct your swing.

If you're hesitant, I probably know why. Like me, you're probably stubbornly holding on to the misguided idea that you need to help the ball up into the air. You might be addressing the ball in your set up position and thinking to yourself: "No way!" As in "there's no way this is going to work. I'm going to hit the top of the golf ball. It will be a 'worm burner.' Or worse, I'll miss the golf ball entirely."

Nope! I'm telling you it's not going to happen. If you don't believe me, I dare you to aim at a spot about an inch in front of the ball and "top" it or miss it completely. If you do it, please send me a video because there's a bigger problem with your golf swing.

It's nearly impossible to swing at a spot about an inch in front of the ball and not hit better, crisper iron shots. When you start striking your iron shots like this, you'll notice a distinctive sound and you'll notice you suddenly have a more penetrating ball flight that adds power and distance to your game!

Before I share the drill that will help you develop and sharpen an iron game that will easily have you breaking 90, let's talk about the bigger picture. Most of the information I shared about the "driver" swing is true about the "iron" swing.

However, the "iron" swing is different in that you most definitely want to strike down on the ball. The "driver" swing is slightly upward if you're using a hybrid, a 5-wood, a 3-wood, or a driver.

The only exception could be if you're using an iron off the tee – and if that's the case you should be working toward at least hitting a hybrid off the tee and working your way up to hitting a driver.

The "hammer to nail" analogy is especially appropriate when it comes to striking crisp irons because much like a hammer striking a nail, with an iron you really will produce the best results by thinking about the golf club as a hammer striking down and through the golf ball as if it were a nail.

THE "GAME CHANGING" IRON STRIKING DRILL

If you'll just practice this drill, it may transform you golf life. However, you can't transform yourself into a great iron player over night – at least if you're mortal like the rest of us. You'll need to start small and work your way up.

Stage 1: Develop the "Feel"

Just like with putting, chipping, and pitching – consider starting with developing the "feel" of striking solid iron shots. Grab a wedge, pick a spot about an inch in front of the ball, trust my advice, and hit the spot.

You'll quickly notice the difference. Your shots will sound different – and better!. The ball flight will improve and you'll notice the added power with which you strike your irons when you use the proper technique.

When you're comfortable – and most likely thrilled – with the results of Stage 1, it's time to move on to…

Stage 2: Distance Control

When you're practicing your game at the driving range, start small by picking a target – and even better a green – about 50 yards out. Strike wedges until you hone in the stroke that consistently produce a shot that hits the green from 50 yards out.

Then move on to 75 yards and repeat the process. Some golfers prefer to use the same swing with a less lofted club while others prefer to use the same club with a bigger swing.

That's a personal preference. By now, you know I don't believe in "one-size-fits-all" solutions. Your task is to find the solution that works best for YOU!

Stage 3: Find Your 100-Yard "Comfort Zone"

Purposely I avoid saying find your 100-yard "club" or your 100-yard "swing" because as I said some golfers prefer a certain club while others prefer a certain swing. You can play good golf and consistently break 90 either way.

By a certain swing, I mean that while some golfers play better by attacking with an aggressive swing, others see better results with a three-quarter swing. And for that reason they may hit say a pitching wedge from 100 yards whereas the aggressive swinger may hit a sand wedge.

The club you hit doesn't matter. What matters is eliminating mis-hits. What matters is having a good idea and being confident that with a certain club and a certain swing the ball will consistently go 100 yards. What matters is hitting your approach shots near the green – and preferably on the green.

And ultimately what really matters when it comes to consistently breaking 90 is putting yourself in the best position to score no worse than a bogey on any particular hole.

When you've found you're 100-yard "comfort zone" move on to…

Stage 4: Find Your 150-Yard "Comfort Zone"

A solidly stuck 7-iron should produce a 150-yard shot from the average golfer. If you can consistently hit a 6-iron 150 yards, great! Just the fact that you can consistently hit greens – or at least leave your approach shots near the green – from 150 yards puts your head and shoulders above most golfers.

And if you can consistently strike an 8-iron such that you're on or near the green from 150 yards, then all the better. That means you have more club speed than the average golfer and provided you can hit the ball fairly straight you have a decided advantage over most golfers.

Work on aiming at a spot about an inch in front of the golf ball and striking down on the ball until you discover the club and the swing that most consistently produces a shot that you can dependably hit 150-yards.

When you can consistently hit the ball 100-yards and 150-yards, it should be fairly simple to either change clubs or adjust your swing to hit the ball various distances like 75-yards, 125-yards, etc.

And if you want to shave strokes off your score then leave your ego on the first tee. Who hasn't heard another golfer brag about how far he hits his pitching wedge – or hasn't done it himself!?!

Who cares if you can hit a pitching wedge 150 yards if you can't do it consistently? Shooting lower scores requires consistency not flashes of greatness.

Breaking 90 consistently means:

• *Consistently* sinking putts inside your "circle of confidence" (and constantly striving to increase the size of your "circle of confidence")
• *Consistently* lagging putts inside your "circle of confidence" – NOT being too aggressive and 3-putting
• *Consistently* leaving "back-half" putts in the back half of your "circle of confidence when you don't sink them – NOT consistently leaving these makeable putts short
• *Consistently* 2-putting greens – NOT sometimes – all the time!
• *Consistently* scoring bogeys (or better) when you fail to hit greens in regulation – NOT "chunking" your chips and pitches or "skulling" them over the greens.
• *Consistently* hitting your drives 200+ yards AND in play – NOT smashing one or two 300 yard drives per round and duck-hooking the others out-of-bounds
• *Consistently* hitting approach shots near the green (if not on the green) – NOT constantly wasting strokes with "mis-hits" like "fat" and "thin" shots
• And *consistently* playing "smart" golf and leaving yourself in the best position to score a bogey or better on every hole – NOT trying to play "hero" shots that leave in a worse position when you don't pull them off – which is most of the time!

The skills you will develop when you dedicate yourself to this simple program for consistently breaking 90 will help you develop a consistent golf game you can count on to reduce your score.

Yet while physical skills are critical, there's a mental skill that may help you more than all the other important skills we've covered. And that is…

ROBERT PHILLIPS

CRITICAL GOLF SKILL #6: PLAY SMART GOLF! (KEEP THE BIG NUMBERS OFF YOUR SCORECARD)

To review the basic plan I revealed at the beginning of this program, on a par 72 course, if you bogey every hole, you'll shoot 90. So to break 90, all you have to do is par one hole – as long as you bogey the rest.

In other words, to break 90 consistently, you need to become just fractionally better than a "bogey golfer."

All you need to do is practice the drills I've shared until you master a few basic golf skills – the critical skills that will help you consistently break 90…

6 Critical Golf Skills for Breaking 90

Critical Golf Skill #1: Consistently 2-putt (Minimize three-putts)

Critical Golf Skill #2: When you miss the green in regulation, pitch or chip the golf ball onto the green (the first time – and of course the nearer the hole the better!)

Critical Golf Skill #3: Turn 3 shots into 2 (Get "up and down" like a PGA pro!)

Critical Golf Skill #4: Consistently hit your tee shots 200 yards or more AND keep them in play! (300-yard drives into the woods won't help you lower your scores.)

Critical Golf Skill #5: Consistently hit approach shots near the green (on the green is even better) and eliminate "mis-hits" like "fat" shots and "thin" shots.

Critical Golf Skill #6:
Keep the big numbers off the card (Play Smart Golf!)

That's it!! Just master a few simple skills and you'll consistently be shooting scores in the 80's. None of it is extraordinary. Those are just basic golf skills anyone of average strength and athleticism can master relatively quickly.

If you can already do all of those things and you're not consistently breaking 90, then you're probably not playing smart golf. You're making bad decisions that add strokes to your score.

You probably just need to improve your course management skill and that's what critical golf skill #6 is all about: shaving strokes off your score by playing smart golf. This will keep the big numbers off your scorecard.

How to play smart golf and lower your scores…

First things first.

Tee It Forward

Before you even tee it up for your first shot, it's important that you play from the appropriate tees. You may not like this (especially if you're a high testosterone male like me!) but if you're going to break 90, you need to play from the tees appropriate to your skill level.

Think about it. If you're a snow skier, do you start on the double-black diamond trail? Only if you have a death wish! You'd be much better off starting on an easier trail – maybe even the "bunny hill" until your skill level improves to the point where you can ski harder trails.

[Note: If you're not familiar with snow skiing, the trails are usually marked to indicate their level of difficulty. The "bunny hill" is the easiest and that's where beginners should start. As your skill level improves you can move on to more difficult slopes that are steeper and have more obstacles like moguls or bumps.

It would be incredibly stupid for a beginner to start on a double-black diamond trail. Those are for accomplished skiers with very high skill levels. A beginner would risk serious injury attempting to ski down such a difficult slope.]

So what does all of this have to do with golf? And with you consistently breaking 90? Plenty!!

Just as the beginner skier shouldn't attempt to ski down a difficult slope, a golfer who can't consistently break 90 should NOT be playing from the "double black diamond" tee boxes set up for scratch or single digit handicap golfers. It's a recipe for frustration, disaster, and triple-digit scores too!

Fortunately golf is not nearly as dangerous as snow skiing so you're not going to kill yourself playing from tee boxes too difficult for your skill level, but you will kill your chances of breaking 90 on a consistent basis.

Golf courses are set up to accommodate the wide variety of golfers with varying degrees of skill depending on what set of tees you play from. You can think of the obstacles on golf courses (like trees, water hazards, and sand traps) as being similar to moguls on a ski slope.

Playing the white tees (or the gold tees if you're a senior golfer or the red tees if you're female golfer) removes some of these obstacles. For example, fairway bunkers and water hazards that may be in play from the blue or black tees may be no problem at all from the white tees.

So if necessary, I recommend you swallow some pride and play from the tee boxes appropriate to your skill level.

OK, enough with my sermon. I'm not your father and I know you're going to play whatever tee boxes you want to play. All I ask is that you at least consider playing the white tees instead of the blue or black tees. Just try it once as a test and see for yourself how it lowers your scores.

Here's a typical scorecard with multiple sets of tees. Some scorecards will even indicate by handicap the skill level recommended for each set of tees but this one does not.

HOLE	Ratings	1	2	3	4	5	6	7	8	9	OUT	10	11	12	13	14	15	16	17	18	IN	TOT	HCP	NET
GOLD	72.4/127	434	389	154	384	391	157	508	415	533	3365	356	475	371	177	455	537	377	203	420	3371	6736		
BLUE	69.8/123	400	366	141	344	357	144	478	372	480	3082	326	464	347	160	415	510	351	175	395	3143	6225		
WHITE	67.9/119 L 73.6/127	384	340	128	324	332	131	453	352	460	2904	310	428	325	140	395	490	335	155	377	2955	5859		
RED																								

Stroke Par	4	4	3	4	4	3	5	4	5	36	4	5	4	3	4	5	4	3	4	36	72
Time Par	:13	:13	:09	:12	:13	:09	:16	:16	:16	1:57	:13	:14	:13	:10	:14	:17	:13	:10	:14	1:58	3:55

GOLD HCP	2	8	18	10	6	16	14	4	12		17	9	13	11	1	5	15	7	3		
BLUE HCP	2	8	18	10	4	16	14	6	12		17	9	13	11	1	5	15	7	3		
WHITE HCP	2	8	18	10	4	16	14	6	12		17	15	9	11	1	5	13	7	3		
RED HCP																					

TEES USED _____ DATE _____
SCORER _____ ATTEST _____

Each course could be set up slightly differently as far as the colors of the tee boxes but typically the back tees (in this case the gold tees) are for the best golfers – usually single digit handicaps who can break 80 consistently. You should NOT be playing these tees.

The next tees (the blues on this scorecard) are for mid-handicap golfers which would be something like 10 to 15. That means these golfers routinely break 90. And since you're not quite at that level yet, it's best to wait until you're breaking 90 consistently to play from these tees.

The white tees are for high handicap golfers. And if you're not consistently breaking 90 yet, then you are a high handicap golfer and you should be playing these tees – at least for now.

The total yardage should be around 6,000 yards total – maybe a bit more or maybe slightly less. In this case, the total yardage of the white tees is 5,859 yards. Perfect!

At this distance, you should have a reasonable expectation of reaching the greens in regulation. Some courses have tees especially for seniors. And of course the red tees are for female golfers.

You may be tempted to play the blue tees, yet if you do you're only making it more difficult to break 90. You will significantly increase your chances of shooting a score in the 80s and having more fun if you tee it up from the white tees.

And that's the whole goal of this book: to provide you with a simple system for breaking 90 on a regular basis. As a matter of fact, it makes so much sense to "tee it forward" that the PGA and USGA launched a "tee it forward" initiative recently.

The program has been a success. Golfers who followed that advice and moved up to the next tee box reported they played faster, had more fun, and will continue to "tee it forward." And let's face it; golf is more fun when you shoot lower scores.

OK, let's move on. Now that you've chosen the set of tees that give you the best chance of breaking 90, let's talk about…

YOUR "PERSONAL PAR"…

As a starting point, take a look at each hole and figure out your "personal par." Par for the course is 72. That's obvious. But you aren't going to par every hole. So let's assign a score you can realistically expect to score on each hole.

There are several ways to do this:

You could just add a stroke to every hole. So every par 3 becomes a par 4, the par 4's are now par 5's, and each par 5 is now a par 6. It all adds up to 90. And to break 90, all you have to do is shoot one better than that. Simple.

You can make adjustments according your skill level. For example, if you think you can reach all the par 3's, then your personal par on those holes is 3. And since now your personal par adds up to 86, you have a 3 stroke "cushion" to play with.

If you're a long hitter, you can make 5 your "personal par" on all the par 5's. It depends on your level of skill and confidence. Unfortunately, I can't make that decision for you.

But if you do need me to make that decision for you, here's a simple solution. Add one stroke to the par of every hole except the easiest hole on the course. Each hole is given a handicap that's shown on the card.

The #1 handicap hole is judged to be the hardest and the #18 handicap hole is judged to be the easiest. In this case, the #18 handicap hole is the third hole from the white tees.

Your "personal par" on hole #3 would be 3 and your "personal par" on every other hole is the regular par plus one.

So your scorecard now looks like this:

Hole	1	2	3	4	5	6	7	8	9	Out	10	11	12	13	14	15	16	17	18	In	Total
Par	4	4	3	4	4	3	5	4	5	36	4	5	4	3	4	5	4	3	4	36	72
Score	5	5	3	5	5	4	6	5	6	44	5	6	5	4	5	6	5	4	5	45	89

If you think you can par all the par 5's, then your scorecard would look like this:

Hole	1	2	3	4	5	6	7	8	9	Out	10	11	12	13	14	15	16	17	18	In	Total
Par	4	4	3	4	4	3	5	4	5	36	4	5	4	3	4	5	4	3	4	36	72
Score	5	5	4	5	5	4	5	5	5	43	5	5	5	4	5	5	5	4	5	43	86

This gives you three shots to play with too. You can score one shot worse than your personal par on any three holes and you'll still break 90. You get the idea.

And now that you've got your "personal par" figured out for each hole and put it in writing, pat yourself on the back. Why? Because you now have a plan in place. You know what you need to score on every hole to break 90. All you need to do to break 90 is execute your plan.

But let me be clear. Just because your "personal par" might be 5 when the regular par is 4, I'm not saying you need to play it as a 3 shot hole (meaning taking 3 shots to reach the green) and then two-putt for a 5 which is your "personal par." Not at all!

It depends on your skill level (mostly your distance) and the length of the hole. Anyone ought to be able to reach a 350-yard hole in two shots. But as the holes get longer, they'll be harder to reach in two shots.

If you can hit a 230-yard drive and 170 yard second shot, then you can reach 400-yard par 4s and you should go for it. On the other hand, if you can hit 200-yard drives and 150 yard second shots, you should play it as a 3 shot hole. Leaving yourself a short pitch shot for your third shot will lead to lower scores than trying to play above your skill level.

But if you're not consistently breaking 90, then you're probably not hitting a lot of greens in regulations. That means you're often pitching or chipping to the green for your third shot. And you can still two-putt for your "personal par."

The extra shot is just a "cushion." If you don't need that cushion that's all the better. Sometimes you'll reach the green in regulation and two-putt for par. And that puts you on track to break 90.

So don't play defensively because your "personal par" is one stroke above regular par. But don't play too aggressively and try to reach long par 4s (or par 5s) in two shots when it's not realistic that you'll reach them. Play it smart, lay up, and leave yourself with an easy shot.

Let's move on...

Don't ruin your round before the 1st hole...

I shouldn't have to say this but before you hit your first tee shot, you will have at least stretched and stroked a few putts to get a feel for the speed of the greens that particular day.

And it would be even better if you hit a few range balls – but I understand there's not always enough time for that. And some courses don't have practice ranges. So at least stretch and stroke a few putts. And hopefully a few chips and pitches too.

Going to the first tee cold is a recipe for disaster. How many times have you gotten off to a slow start on the first few holes and then started playing well when you got loose?

Plus getting double-bogeys (or worse) on the first couple holes certainly does not put you on the most positive mental state. Some golfers let getting off to a slow start ruin their entire round.

Don't let that happen to you. Warm-up before your round. Stretch, stroke some putts, and hit some range balls.

Play within yourself

Golfers get themselves in trouble when they play too aggressively. You don't need to be "hero" and hit 250 or 300 yards drives to break 90. You don't have to attack pins to break 90. All you need to do is execute the plan you've already written down on your scorecard.

Playing "within yourself" means accepting that you can consistently hit a 200-yard drive and keep it in play or a 225-yard drive and keep it in play. It also means you recognize that when you over swing and try to get an extra 25 yards out of your drive bad things happen.

That's when your duck hook or slice suddenly reappears. That's when you put yourself in trouble and that's when your scores quickly soar above your "personal par." And if you keep pressing for the entire round, that's when your score skyrockets over 90.

Playing "within yourself" means hitting a 3-wood, 5-wood, or hybrid club off the tee because that's the club that keeps the ball in play. What's the point of hitting a 250-yard drive if it ends up in trouble most of the time? You'd be better off (and shoot lower scores) hitting a 3-wood 225 or a 5-wood 200 and keeping it in play.

When selecting an iron, take one more club if you have to. For example, instead of crushing your 8-iron or 9-iron 150, take a smooth swing with your 7-iron. You get the same score no matter what club you hit so play the "smart" club. Just play "within yourself" and the desired results will follow.

Play Smart to Give Yourself the Best Chance to Succeed…

Like I said, you don't need to be overly aggressive to break 90, you just need to execute your plan. Shoot for the middle of the green, not for the pin on your approach shots.

When you get into trouble, as you occasionally will, get out of trouble with your next shot. Just put the ball back in play and go from there. Don't try to be a hero. Don't think you're Phil Mickelson if you can't break 90 consistently. Phil can pull off "miracle shots" but even Phil gets himself in more trouble when he doesn't execute the "hero shot."

And that's the problem. More often than not, instead of pulling off the great shot you envisioned, you screw it up and put yourself in an even worse spot.

Golf guru Dave Pelz has done extensive research that shows most golfers play below their handicap for most of their rounds. But they "blow up" on two or three holes and that's what explodes their scores.

Playing "smart" may not eliminate "blow up" holes entirely but it will reduce your chances of scoring a 7, 8, or higher on any single hole.

Play away from hazards like water and bunkers or sand traps when it makes sense. Think about it. If your "personal par" is a bogey, then all you need to do is get the ball near the green in two shots (or in three shots on a par 5). Then you just chip it on the green, two-putt and walk off the green with your "personal par" – one hole closer to breaking 90.

Playing "smart" and playing "within yourself" goes a long way toward keeping big numbers off your scorecard and ultimately shooting scores in the 80's.

The 3 Options Rule

With nearly every shot, you can come up with at least 3 options for how to play it and probably more. Think about the best 3 options for playing each shot and then eliminate the two most risky options. This leaves you with the safest option as the way you'll play the shot. Some examples will be helpful.

Let's say there's a tee shot on a par 5 with a water hazard. It takes a 200-yard carry to clear the water. In other words, if you're ball flies any distance less than 200-yards – even 190-yards – you'll end up wet and have to take a penalty stroke and hit 3 off the tee.

You know you're capable of clearing the water with your driver. Yet you also know you only hit the ball that well half the time. The "smart" play is to lay up short of the water and play this particular par 5 as a three shot hole – three shots to reach the green. I realize that was only two options – not three – but you get the idea.

I can't possibly go through every potential scenario you'll encounter on the golf course. Just think about your options before each shot. Maybe the three options are three different types of shots. The three options could be three different clubs that you could hit. Or it could be three distances.

Just know your ability, your strengths and weaknesses, and use your head. Play the option that gives you the best chanced to succeed. And for our purposes, we define success on each hole as a bogey (or said another way – keeping the high numbers off your scorecard). Play the hole in the manner that gives you the best chance of success under the circumstances.

Play One Hole at a Time…

You often hear athletes talk about playing one game at a time or playing one play at a time. What they mean is that they play a whole season in one game. Losing one game doesn't ruin the season. And messing up one play probably won't lose the game.

Applying this concept to golf, you can't break 90 in one hole. And just because you have one bad hole, doesn't mean you can't still break 90. You can score a stroke or two over your "personal par" on a hole and still break 90. Sure, it will be more challenging because you're going to have to make up those lost strokes but it can be done.

Don't lose faith because of one bad shot or one bad hole. Even professional golfers hit bad shots. They just recover and move on from those bad shots. And you should do the same.

Yet there's a big difference between a professional and a high handicapper. PGA pros cannot only get out of trouble; they can routinely hit extraordinary recovery shots and hit greens from the most unlikely places.

Players with less skill, like you and me, should look for the easiest way to get the ball back in play such that they still have a chance to score their "personal par" on the hole. Just punch it back into the fairway if that's all you've got.

Remain focused on the shot at hand. Don't get caught up in the negative emotions of one bad hole and don't look too far forward to the holes in front of you.

Focus your energy and attention on the shot you're taking at the moment. Yet before you hit each shot think about the next shot. In other words…

Play the Hole Backwards…

You may find it helpful to play the hole backwards. All that means is think about your next shot and where you'd like to hit it from, then hit your current shot to that spot.

For example, let's say you're playing a 370-yard hole. It's a par 4 but your "personal par" is 5. And let's say you feel really comfortable hitting an

8-iron from 140 yards out. Knowing that, you need to hit a 230yard drive (370 yards less 230 yard drive leaves 140 yards to the pin).

Now let's say you hit your tee shot a bit "fat" so you hit it 215-yards and even push it a bit right (assuming you're a right-handed golfer) into the rough. Let's also say the pin is tucked behind a bunker on the right side of an elevated green, there's another greenside bunker to the right, and if you go long you're out-of-bounds in the trees.

What do you do? The dumb play is to "attack" the pin. Unless you're a low-handicap golfer, you have no business even thinking about attacking that pin. That brings all kinds of bad things into play.

Instead of hitting a great shot and having a birdie putt, the more likely outcome – given that you're a high-handicap golfer – is that your next shot will either be in the bunker or if you don't end up in the bunker, you'll be "short-sided" meaning you won't have much green to work with for your next shot so it will be difficult to chip the ball close to the hole.

Now you've brought a score of 6 or higher into play. Not smart!! The "smart play is aim to the center or even left side of the green. Remember, your "personal par" is 5.

If you put it on the green, you can three-putt and still score a 5 – your "personal par." Or even better, you could two-putt for a real par. And if you're not on the green with your second shot, when you aim left of the pin to avoid trouble, you leave yourself a much easier chip shot with a lot more green to work with.

It will be infinitely easier to chip the ball on the green and two-putt for your personal par than it would be to do the same thing from either the sand trap or from a "short-sided" lie.

By playing each hole backwards, you're actually thinking one shot ahead. And as you can clearly see that will save you strokes and help you break 90. And that's the short story.

Let's recap:

Step #1: Select the tees appropriate for your skill level to increase your chances of breaking 90. On most courses, these will be the white tees and the total yardage should be about 6,000 yards.

Step #2: Decide on your "personal par" for each hole. They should all add up to a score of 89 or less. That's your blueprint for breaking 90. Now all that's left is to execute that plan.

Here are a few tips to help you execute your plan:

Tip #1: Warm-up before your round. Stretch and stroke a few putts to get a feel for the speed of the greens. Hit some range balls. Getting loose before you hit your first tee shot can help get you off to a fast start that puts you in a positive frame of mind the entire round.

Tip #2: Play "within yourself." Play "smart." Don't be a "hero." Don't over swing in an effort to hit the ball farther. Play the safe shot. Don't try shots you're not likely to execute. Avoid danger. Play away from hazards like water and sand traps.

Tip #3: Play one hole at a time. You can't break 90 in one hole. And one bad hole won't kill you. Stay focused on your goal. You can make up a few strokes later in the round.

Tip #4: Play each hole backwards. Before hitting your current shot, think about your next shot and where you'd like to hit it from in terms of both distance and position (left of the green or right of the green). If you miss your first putt, leave it close enough to make the second-putt.

If your favorite distance is 120-yards and you're teeing off on a 350-yard hole, try to hit a 230-yard drive. Play away from hazards (trees, water, bunkers) on your approach shots to give yourself a better chance to chip on the green and two-putt for your "personal par."

The point is to think about your next shot before hitting your current shot. Then hit the shot that puts you in the best position to walk off the green with your "personal par."

You'll discover more thoughts and helpful ideas on the best ways to play each type of hole – par 3's, par 4's, and par 5's – as well as how to shave the single stroke of your score that could help a bogey golfer break 90 in the Appendixes.

Start playing "smart" golf and you'll increase your chances of breaking 90. And when you do, I want to hear about it.

Tell me about your success and help inspire other golfers to break 90 too. Email me at <u>robert@golfaggressive.com</u>.

At this point, you should a solid idea about how you can break 90. Now let's work on a flexible practice plan for breaking 90 as quickly as possible. We'll start with the most critical skills – the short game skills – before moving on to the other critical skills.

There will be specific goals to achieve every week and each week will build on the previous week. That gives you more practice and more time to develop confidence in the areas that will help you lower your scores fastest: putting, chipping, and pitching.

THE GAME PLAN: HOW TO BREAK 90 IN 42 DAYS OR LESS...

Congratulations! You've made it this far. You know the 6 critical golf skills you need to develop and you know the practice drills that will help you develop those critical golf skills.

Now it's time to see how serious you are about consistently breaking 90. Remember, at the very beginning I said I am as serious about helping you consistently break 90 as quickly as possible as you are about achieving that goal.

So how serious are you? Are you ready to get started with a practice plan that can help you shoot scores in the 80 in 42 days – just 6 short weeks from today?

If you answered, "yes," then let's get started!

As you'll see, I've created a weekly practice plan for you. It's a list of things for you to accomplish each week. Each week builds on the previous week. It doesn't matter when or how often you practice. I understand everyone has a different schedule. That's why I've created flexible practice schedule.

All that matters is that you accomplish the goals each and every week. Whether you do it in a single day, over the weekend, or over the course of the entire week isn't as important as practicing and accomplishing the goals.

As the days and weeks pass, you'll gain confidence and momentum as you see and track your progress. And most importantly, you'll be developing the critical golf skill you'll need to break 90 – not just once, but practically every time you tee it up for a round of golf!

You also need to keep track of your progress so you can clearly see how your golf game is steadily improving and how you are making progress in developing the critical golf skills necessary to consistently break 90.

If you've read the entire book these goals will be self-explanatory so I'm not going to waste your time rehashing what I've already written. You can always go back and re-read the previous sections. I've covered each of the 6 critical golf skill and the practice drills in detail.

So print out your "Break 90 Practice Plan and Progress Tracker" and get started!

Week #1: Short Game – Putting

The first week is all about putting because sinking more putts is the single fastest way to lower your scores. Go back and review the drills I shared earlier if necessary, then start practicing so you can develop the skills.

Remember, you can probably do these drills at home so there really are no excuses. And the sooner you start practicing, the faster you'll improve your skills, and the faster you'll break 90.

Here are the goals for Week #1: Keep track of your progress on the progress tracking sheets provided in Appendix D.

Week #1: Skills Test & Practice Goals

Skills Test: Assess your putting

#1: Stroke 25 3-foot putts and keep track of how many you make…

#2: Stroke 25 "lag" putts and keep track of how many you leave inside your "COC"

PRESSURE Test: On the "lag" putts, stroke the 2nd putt and keep track of how many times you 2-putt

This is your baseline. Your goal is to improve these results every week.

Practice Goals

Goal #1: Sink 100 3-foot putts to create a 3-foot "circle of confidence"
Goal #2: "Lag" 50 putts of 15'+ inside a 3' "COC" (BONUS Goal: make the 2nd putt!)
Goal #3: "Lag" 50 putts of 10' to 15' inside the back half of a 3' "COC" – in other words, don't leave them short! (BONUS Goal: make the 2nd putt!)

Week #2: Keep Putting. Add Pitching and Chipping

Remember, each week will build on skills developed the previous week. In Week #2, you'll keep developing your putting skills and add pitching and chipping to develop a complete short game.

You'll have the same putting goals every week for the entire program so your putting skills should really improve over the course of six weeks – provided you make the effort to practice and achieve the goals every week.

In addition to putting, I've added two new goals for pitching and chipping. Go back and review the section on chipping and putting if necessary, then start practicing the drills and improving your skills.

Here are the goals for Week #2: Keep track of your progress on the progress tracking sheets provided in Appendix D.

Week #2: Skills Tests & Practice Goals

Skills Test #1: Putting Test

Stroke 25 3-foot putts and keep track of how many you make…

Stroke 25 "lag" putts and keep track of how many you leave inside your "COC"

PRESSURE TEST: On the "lag" putts, stroke the 2nd putt and keep track of how many times you hole the 2nd putt

Did you improve from last week? Keep track of your progress

Skills Test #2: Assess your chipping

Take 25 chip shots of various lengths and leave them inside a 15 foot circle surrounding the hole.

PRESSURE TEST: Putt out the chips. Keep track of how many times you get "up and down" and how many times you 2-putt.

This is your baseline. Your goal is to improve these results every week.

Practice Goals

Goal #1: Sink 100 3-foot putts to create a 3-foot "circle of confidence"
Goal #2: "Lag" 50 putts of 15'+ inside a 3' "COC" (extra credit: make the 2nd putt!)
Goal #3: "Lag" 50 putts of 10' to 15' inside the back half of a 3' "COC" –

in other words, don't leave them short! (BONUS Goal: make the 2nd putt!)

Goal #4: Chip 100 shots of various distances inside a 15 foot circle around the hole (BONUS Goal: putt out the chip shots with the goal of 2-putting or better)

Week #3: Getting Off the Tee

After two weeks of honing your short game skills, you should be seeing some improvement – especially with your putting. In Week #3, we'll continue working to improve the short game and we'll add the critical skill of getting off the tee.

You have the same putting, chipping, and pitching goals from the previous two weeks. And we'll add the long game to the mix because while getting off the tee may not be as important to breaking 90 as the short game, it's still a critical skill.

Remember, the goal is NOT to swing wildly and see how far you can hit the ball. Without a doubt hitting longer tee shots will help lower your scores. Yet what most golfers seem to forget is that consistency is more important than distance.

Bombing 300-yard drives is of little use if you can't consistently keep the ball in play. The goal is to find the club you can consistently hit at least 200 yards off the tee while keeping it in play.

If that club is a 3-wood, a 5-wood, a hybrid, or some other club instead of your driver, then keep the driver in the bag until you can consistently keep it in play.

The goal is to hit 15 of 20 drives 200 yards AND in play. That's 75% and that's a good start. When you get to 75%, challenge yourself to increase that to 80% (16 of 20), 85% (17 of 20), 90% (18 of 20), and even 100%. The more confidence you have when you step up to the tee, the better.

By keeping your drives in play, all I mean is that while you're practicing at the driving range, aim at a specific target and honestly judge whether or not the golf ball ended up in what you know to be the bounds of the normal width of a fairway. You can add a few yards on either side because even if your drive is in the rough, it's still in play as long as you're not blocked out by trees or anything else.

As you improve you want to hit more fairways of course. However, for the purposes of consistently breaking 90, just keeping your tee shots in play is good enough. All that means is having a clear second shot.

Here are the goals for Week #3: Keep track of your progress on the progress tracking sheets provided in Appendix D.

Week #3: Skills Tests & Practice Goals

Skills Test #1: Putting Test

Stroke 25 3-foot putts and keep track of how many you make…

Stroke 25 "lag" putts and keep track of how many you leave inside your "COC"

BONUS TEST: On the "lag" putts, stroke the 2nd putt and keep track of how many times you hole the 2nd putt

Did you improve from last week? Keep track of your progress

Skills Test #2: Assess your chipping

Take 25 chip shots of various lengths and leave them inside a 15 foot circle surrounding the hole.

PRESSURE TEST: Putt out the chips. Keep track of how many times you get "up and down" and how many times you 2-putt.

Did you improve from last week? Keep track of your progress.

Skills Test #3: Hitting Tee Shots 200+ Yards AND Keeping Them in Play

Take 25 tee shots and keep track of how many you hit at least 200 yards and keep in play.

This is your baseline. Your goal is to improve these results every week.

Practice Goals

Goal #1: Sink 100 3-foot putts to create a 3-foot "circle of confidence"
Goal #2: "Lag" 50 putts of 15'+ inside a 3' "COC" (extra credit: make the

2nd putt!)
Goal #3: "Lag" 50 putts of 10' to 15' inside the back half of a 3' "COC" – in other words, don't leave them short! (BONUS Goal: make the 2nd putt!)
Goal #4: Chip 100 shots of various distances inside a 15 foot circle around the hole (BONUS Goal: putt out the chip shots with the goal of 2-putting or better)
Goal #5: Practice your tee shots with the goal of hitting at least 15 out of 20 200+ yards AND in play.

Week #4: Short Irons and Approach Shots

This week we'll add irons to the mix because eliminating mis-hits with the irons could be the key to lowering your scores. Many high-handicap golfers lose countless strokes to poor iron play.

Sure, you'd like to hit more greens in regulation and you should strive to do that. Yet eliminating the "fat" shots, the "chunk" shots, the "worm burner" ground balls, and the "thin" line drives may be where high-handicap golfers can save the most strokes when it comes to the iron game.

Being able to consistently hit greens from 100-yards and in will help lower your scores so in addition to putting, chipping, and tee shots, we'll add some drills for short-irons this week too.

The goal this week is to find your 100-yard "comfort zone." Please go back and review the section on short-irons if necessary. However finding your 100-yard "comfort zone" simply means finding the combination of the club and the swing that gives you the most confidence in consistently hitting the golf ball 100-yards.

When you develop this skill, you'll take that confidence to the golf course and increase your chances of hitting greens from 100-yards out. If you're really serious about breaking 90 however, don't stop at finding your 100-yard "comfort zone."

Find your comfort zones from various distances such as 50-yards, 75-yards, 125-yards, etc. The more comfortable you are from various distances, the more greens you'll hit. And that should lead to the lower golf scores you seek.

Here are the goals for Week #4: Keep track of your progress on the progress tracking sheets provided in Appendix D.

Week #4: Skills Tests & Practice Goals

Skills Test #1: Putting Test

Stroke 25 3-foot putts and keep track of how many you make...

Stroke 25 "lag" putts and keep track of how many you leave inside your "COC"

Extra Credit: On the "lag" putts, stroke the 2nd putt and keep track of how many times you hole the 2nd putt

Did you improve from last week? Keep track of your progress

Skills Test #2: Assess your chipping

Take 25 chip shots of various lengths and leave them inside a 15 foot circle surrounding the hole.

PRESSURE TEST: Putt out the chips. Keep track of how many times you get "up and down" and how many times you 2-putt.

Did you improve from last week? Keep track of your progress.

Skills Test #3: Hitting Tee Shots 200+ Yards AND Keeping Them in Play

Take 25 tee shots and keep track of how many you hit at least 200 yards and keep in play.

Did you improve from last week? Keep track of your progress.

Skills Test #4: Hitting 100-yard Iron Shots on (or near) the Green

Hit 25 iron shots to a target 100-yards away. Keep track of how many hit the green (or would have hit the green if you don't have a green to shoot for).

This is your baseline. Your goal is to improve these results every week.

Practice Goals

Goal #1: Sink 100 3-foot putts to create a 3-foot "circle of confidence"

Goal #2: "Lag" 50 putts of 15'+ inside a 3' "COC" (extra credit: make the 2nd putt!)

Goal #3: "Lag" 50 putts of 10' to 15' inside the back half of a 3' "COC" – in other words, don't leave them short! (BONUS Goal: make the 2nd putt!)

Goal #4: Chip 100 shots of various distances inside a 15-foot circle around the hole (BONUS Goal: putt out the chip shots with the goal of 2-putting or better)

Goal #5: Practice your tee shots with the goal of hitting at least 15 out of 20 200+ yards AND in play.

Goal #6: Practice your 100-yard iron shots until you can hit the green 15 out 20 times. (If you don't have a green as a target, use your best judgment.)

Week #5: Adding Mid-Irons to the Mix

At this point, you've been practicing and improving your short game skills for a solid month. You're confidence should be increasing every week.

You've also been working on your tee shots for a few weeks. By now you should have found the club you can consistently hit at least 200 yards AND keep in play.

And last week, we added the link between getting off the tee and hitting your approach shots near the green (or even on the green) where your stellar short game will get the ball into the hole in as few strokes as possible.

This week we'll build on those skill by adding the mid-iron and finding your "comfort zone" from 150-yards so you can get approach shots from this distance either on or near the green.

Finding a "comfort zone" from 150-yards is a good start, yet the best golfers don't stop there. To increase your golf skills – and your chances of breaking 90 – work on finding a "comfort zone" from other mid-iron distances such as 125-yards, 175-yards, and distances in between.

Here are the goals for Week #5: Keep track of your progress on the progress tracking sheets provided in Appendix D.

Week #5: Skills Tests & Practice Goals

Skills Test #1: Putting Test

Stroke 25 3-foot putts and keep track of how many you make…

Stroke 25 "lag" putts and keep track of how many you leave inside your "COC"

PRESSURE TEST: On the "lag" putts, stroke the 2nd putt and keep track of how many times you hole the 2nd putt

Did you improve from last week? Keep track of your progress

Skills Test #2: Assess your chipping

Take 25 chip shots of various lengths and leave them inside a 15 foot circle surrounding the hole.

PRESSURE TEST: Putt out the chips. Keep track of how many times you get "up and down" and how many times you 2-putt.

Did you improve from last week? Keep track of your progress.

Skills Test #3: Hitting Tee Shots 200+ Yards AND Keeping Them in Play

Take 25 tee shots and keep track of how many you hit at least 200 yards and keep in play.

Did you improve from last week? Keep track of your progress.

Skills Test #4: Hitting 100-yard Iron Shots on (or near) the Green

Hit 25 iron shots to a target 100-yards away. Keep track of how many hit the green (or would have hit the green if you don't have a green to shoot for).

Did you improve from last week? Keep track of your progress.

Skills Test #5: Hitting 150-yard Iron Shots on (or near) the Green

Hit 25 iron shots to a target 150-yards away. Keep track of how many hit the green (or would have hit the green if you don't have a green to shoot for).

This is your baseline. Your goal is to improve these results every week.

Practice Goals

Goal #1: Sink 100 3-foot putts to create a 3-foot "circle of confidence"
Goal #2: "Lag" 50 putts of 15'+ inside a 3' "COC" (extra credit: make the 2nd putt!)
Goal #3: "Lag" 50 putts of 10' to 15' inside the back half of a 3' "COC" – in other words, don't leave them short! (BONUS Goal: make the 2nd putt!)
Goal #4: Chip 100 shots of various distances inside a 15-foot circle around the hole (BONUS Goal: putt out the chip shots with the goal of 2-putting or better)
Goal #5: Practice your tee shots with the goal of hitting at least 15 out of 20 200+ yards AND in play.
Goal #6: Practice your 100-yard iron shots until you can hit the green or near the green 15 out 20 times. (If you don't have a green as a target, use your best judgment.)
Goal #7: Practice your 150-yard iron shots until you can hit the green or near the green 15 out 20 times. (If you don't have a green as a target, use your best judgment.)

Week #6: Putting It All Together: Play Smart Golf and Break 90!

If you've been diligent in your practice, you can't help but to have improved both your golf skills and your confidence level over the past 5 weeks. You have the skills to break 90. Now it's time to do it!

Seriously…

- ✓ If you can *consistently* make putts inside a 3-foot "circle of confidence"…

- ✓ If you can *consistently* lag 15-foot putts inside a 3-foot "circle of confidence"…

- ✓ If you can *consistently* either sink or leave all putts between 3' and 15' in the back half of the COC…

- ✓ If you can *consistently* chip and pitch the ball into a 15-foot circle around the hole…

- ✓ If you can *consistently* hit your drives 200+ yards AND keep them in play…

- ✓ If you can *consistently* hit 100-yard approach shots on or near the green…

- ✓ If you can *consistently* hit 150-yard approach shots on or near the green…

- ✓ If you *consistently* make smart course management decisions that keep big numbers off your scorecard…

If you have developed the golf skills to do all this forget 90! You might be breaking 80!!!

If you haven't developed all of these skills, then after 5 weeks of practice, you know where your weak spots are so focus your practice on those areas.

And keep practicing and tracking your improvement in all areas of the game: putting, pitching, chipping, tee shots, approach shots, and course management.

It's time to hit the course and break 90. However, before you hit your first tee shot you may want to review the section on critical golf skill #6 about playing smart and thinking one shot ahead.

And if you want a simple strategy for scoring a bogey on every hole see Appendix A. It ought to be a piece of cake if you've developed the six critical golf skills I've covered.

And if you haven't developed all of these golf skills, then keep working and practicing. As long as you are committed, success is just around the corner because here is…

ROBERT PHILLIPS

THE STRANGEST SECRET

Many years ago Earl Nightingale released a CD called "The Strangest Secret." It could have been in the 1960s or it may have been even earlier. I'm sure you can find the CD with a simple Internet search.

In any event, Earl took about an hour to layout "The Strangest Secret." It's a tried and true success secret. And don't worry, I won't make you wait an hour to hear the secret. I'll just spill the beans right now.

Earl Nightingale said "The Strangest Secret" is this: You become what you think about.

It makes sense if you think about it. What do you think about? If you think about becoming a great salesman, then you probably practice sales pitches and study sales tactics. And if you have the dedication and commitment to keep at it, you eventually will become a great salesman.

The same is true of your golf game. If you're truly serious about breaking 90, then you probably think about it quite a bit. And if that's the case, your dedication and commitment will lead you to practice diligently until you improve your skills to the degree necessary to consistently break 90. It's as simple as that.

The simple plan is laid out for you right here in these pages. It absolutely does not take any great strength or athletic skill to become a golfer good enough to consistently break 90. And if you're really committed to achieving the goal, you should be able to achieve it in a relatively short period of time.

Research has proven it helps to put your goal in writing. If nothing else, the simple act of putting goals in writing is like making a contract with yourself. You've committed yourself to achieving a goal and you're more likely to achieve the goal when you put it in writing.

You're even more likely to achieve the goal if you strategically share your goal with people who you trust to hold you accountable.

With that in mind, I encourage you to print out the following "commitment page," sign it, and post it in a place where you'll see it every day.

And that's it! You have all the information you need to be breaking 90 soon. The question is do you have the determination and commitment to follow through and achieve your goal. If you're still with me, then I'm betting you do!

If you have any questions or a success story you would like to share, please email me at robert@golfaggressive.com.

MY COMMITMENT TO BREAK 90 WITHIN THE NEXT 42 DAYS…

I am committed to breaking 90 within the next 42 days. I will break 90 within the next 42 days.

I am dedicating the next 42 days to achieving this goal. I promise to practice diligently to develop the critical skills necessary to consistently break 90.

Specifically, over the next 42 days I will…

- Sink 100 3-foot putts every week to create a 3-foot "circle of confidence"
- "Lag" 50 putts of 15'+ inside a 3' COC every week
- Successfully stroke 50 "back-half" putts either into the hole or leave them in the back-half of the COC every week
- Chip 25 shots inside a 15' COC every week
- Pitch 25 shots inside a 15' COC every week
- Practice my tee shots until I can consistently hit 15 out of every 20 drives 200+ yards AND keep them in play
- Find my 100-yard "comfort zone" to develop the confidence to hit more greens with my short irons (and leave the golf ball near the green when I miss the green so that I can chip or pitch the ball on to the green and 2-putt)
- Find my 150-yard "comfort zone" to develop the confidence to hit more greens with my middle irons (and leave the golf ball near the green when I miss the green so that I can chip or pitch the ball on to the green and 2-putt)
- Play smart golf
- Play the tees appropriate to my skill level to give me the best chance of breaking 90
- Play each hole backwards and think one shot ahead to avoid making costly mistakes that cost me strokes
- Keep track of my progress so I can see the improvement in my golf game

---------------------------------   -----------------------------   --------------
Printed Name   Signature   Date

APPENDIX A: PROVEN 2-STEP GAME PLAN FOR BREAKING 90

Step #1: Score a bogey or better on every hole…

Step #2: Eliminate a single stroke from "bogey" golf…

Here's a simple strategy for bogeying ever hole on the golf course (or better)…

Par 4's

These holes are designed to be played in 4 shots: the tee shot, the approach shot, and two putts.

Here's the simple strategy for scoring a bogey 5 on these holes.

Shot #1: Hit your tee shot at least 200 yards and in play.

Shot #2: Hit your approach shot near the green. I'm not saying to intentionally play away from the green. You should try to put your approach shot on the green and if you do all the better.

However, players who struggle to break 90 consistently typically mis-hit many shots throughout the round. The most common being "fat shots" where you hit the ground before you hit the ball and lose distance. And "thin shots" where you top the ball and hit a low ground ball.

That being the case, you want to work toward eliminating these mishits that cost you strokes. Of course we will work toward hitting as many greens in regulation in possible but it's not going to happen overnight. We'll do it in steps, and the first step is to develop the confidence and skill to consistently make good contact with the ball and get it at least near the green.

By near the green, I mean close enough that you're next shot is a pitch or chip shot. From there your short game skills take over.

Shot #3: Chip or pitch the ball on to the green. If you're practicing the drills I shared earlier, you should be able to either pitch or chip the ball on to the green with ease.

Shots #4 & #5: Then you two-putt, pick the ball up out of the hole, jot down the "5" on your score card and move on to the next tee. Simple as that. And if you either hit the green in regulation or chip or pitch the ball inside your "circle of confidence," then you ought to 2-putt for par.

Par 3's

These holes are designed to be played in 3 shots: the tee shot and two putts.

Here's the simple bogey strategy on par 3's:

Shot #1: Hit your tee shot near the green at worst. Try to hit the green but play away from any danger like water, bunkers, or other hazards that may cost you a shot like woods or weeds that put you out-of-bounds.

Just to be clear, I'm not recommending playing away from the green so that you can then chip or pitch your next shot on to the green. Not at all!

In fact, hitting the green in in regulation on short par 3s and then two-putting for par is a great way to shave the one or two strokes off your score that help you break 90.

However, it's a fact that golfers who can't consistently break 90 do not hit many "greens in regulation." That just means hitting the green with your tee shot on a par 3, with your second shot on a par 4, and with your third shot on a par 5. If you hit the green in regulation, then you should be able to two-putt for par.

And since golfers who can't break 90 don't hit many greens in regulations, you'll lower your scores by at least getting your approach shots near the green so you can pitch or chip your next shot on to the green and two-putt for bogey.

What that really means is minimizing – and hopefully eliminating – costly mishits like "fat" shots and "thin" or "topped" shots. Fat shots happen when you hit the ground before you hit the ball. Thin or topped shots happen when you strike the top of the ball. The result is usually a ground ball or a low line drive.

Either way – "fat" or "thin" – these mishits end up costing you strokes. I'll give you some drills that will help you strike the ball better and reduce these costly mishits.

For now, I just wanted to make the point that the best way for a high-handicap golfer to reduce his score is probably NOT to think about hitting more greens but rather to eliminate mishits and other common mistakes that cost you strokes.

Hitting more greens in regulation certainly should lower your score but let's save that for when you're trying to break 80. For now focusing on eliminating mishits and at least hitting your approach shots near the green will help you break 90.

Shot #2: Pitch or chip your second shot on to the green.

Shots #3 & #4: Now that you are on the green, just 2-putt for your 4. And again, if you either hit the green in regulation or chip or pitch the ball inside your "circle of confidence," then you ought to 2-putt for par.

Par 5's

These longer holes are designed to be played in 5 shots: the tee shot, the fairway shot, the approach shot, and two putts.

If you're either a long hitter or exceptionally good with your short irons, there's no reason you can't stand on the tee box and expect to par these holes. And that goes a long way toward helping you break 90.

That's a personal decision. Only you know whether or not you're a long-hitter or if you have the ability to consistently hit greens from about 100 yards out.

However, even if you're not a long-hitter, par 5's can present the best opportunities for knocking a stroke off your score – as long as you play smart!

Think about it this way. From the white tees, par 5's are probably no longer than 500-yards. So if you can hit a 225-yard drive followed by a 175-yard second shot, that leaves you 100-yards out for your approach shot.

So effectively what you've done is turn this into a 100-yard par 3 because if you hit the green with your 100-yard approach shot, then 2-putt, you'll walk off the green with a par 5.

Thinking about that way should help you par one or two par 5's and those could be the precious strokes that help you break 90. In any event, here's the simple strategy for scoring a bogey 6 on every par 5:

Shot #1: Hit your tee shot at least 200 yards and in play.

Shot #2: If you're a long-hitter and you're confident you can either reach the green in two shots OR if you miss the green leave yourself with an easy pitch or chip shot, then go for it.

However, before you pull the 3-wood or 5-wood out of your bag, think about the next shot. Think about the potential risk versus the potential reward and be honest with yourself.

Ask yourself if going for the green really a risk worth taking. Are you really confident you can consistently either hit the green with this shot OR leave yourself with a pitch or chip if you miss the green?

If the answer is yes, then go for it. If the reality is that half the time you use these long clubs you hit a 50-yard "worm burner" and leave yourself with another long shot for your third shot. Or if you tend to hook or slice shots with your woods and long irons, then keep the long-iron or wood in the bag and play a smart second shot.

If you decide to play a "smart" second shot – which is probably what you really should do – then think one shot ahead. What's your favorite distance? If you feel confident hitting approach shots from 100-yards out, then do the math and hit the shot that leaves you in your comfort zone.

For example, if you're 260-yards out, hit a 160-yard shot that leaves you 100-yards out.

Shot #3: The long hitters who hit their second shots near the green ought to be able to chip or pitch the ball on to the green and 2-putt for par. However, that's not most golfers who can't consistently break 90.

The golfers who laid up with a "smart" second shot should be at a comfortable distance where they feel confident in hitting the green or at worst leaving the ball close to the green where they can pitch or chip.

Shot #4: If you're not already on the green, the fourth shot should be a pitch or chip on to the green.

Shots #5 & #6: Once you're on the green you ought to be able to 2-putt for bogey – or even par if you reached the green in regulation or pitched or chipped the ball inside your circle of confidence.

And now for step #2…

How to Eliminate A Single Shot From Your Round of Bogey Golf

Eliminating the single shot that allows you to break 90 is simple. Over the course of 18 holes, you're going to have several "green light" opportunities to shave a stroke off your score.

It could be on one of the par 3's. If you hit just one of the greens in regulation and two-putt, there's your stroke. Or it could be on one of the 14 approach shots you have on the par 4's and par 5's. If you can hit just one of those 14 greens in regulation (and I have full confidence that you can hit more than one green!) and two-putt, there's your stroke.

Note: Greens in regulation (or GIR) is a term that means your golf ball is on the putting service "in regulation." Since par for every hole is two putts. You just subtract 2 from par for the hole to determine how many strokes you have to "hit the green in regulation."

If your ball is on the green after one shot on par 3's, two shots on par 4's, or three shots on par 5's, then you've hit the green in regulation. Now all you need to do is two-putt for par. The more GIRs you have, the lower your score ought to be. Hitting one or two greens in regulation and 2-putting for par could be the difference between shooting 91 and shooting 89.

As you develop your short game skills, you'll start eliminating strokes too. It's common sense that the more you practice your pitching and chipping and the better you get, the closer you'll be putting the ball to the hole. And that means more one-putts.

As you can see, you'll have plenty of opportunities to shave off the single stroke that reduces your score to 89 or even better.

ROBERT PHILLIPS

APPENDIX B: QUESTIONS & ANSWERS

Here are the answers to some commonly asked questions:

Q: What tees should you play?

A: If you can't break 90, you should NOT be playing the back tees. Those tees are designed for single digit handicappers and if you can't break 90, you're obviously not a single digit handicapper, right?

So let's be honest, to give yourself the best chance of shooting the lowest score you should be playing from the tees designed for your skill level. Not all courses are the same but typically golf courses have 3 or 4 different tee boxes.

The black or blue tees: These are for single-digit handicappers. The distance is usually 6,500 yards or more – way too long for a golfer who can't break 90 consistently. You cannot reasonably expect to break 100 from these tees, let alone 90. You should NOT be playing from these tees that are set up for golfers of a higher skill level.

The white tees: These are the tees set up for mid to high handicappers and these are the tees you should be playing (unless you are a senior or a lady). The total yardage is typically about 6,000 yards give or take a few hundred yards.

The red tees: These are the tees set up for women.

The gold tees: These are usually called the "senior" tees. So if you're a senior, you can play these tees. Or if you're a particularly short hitter, you may also want to play these tees until you add more power and distance to your game. I'd say if you can't consistently hit your tee shots 200 yards or more, then you should consider playing these tees.

Q: What clubs should I have in my bag?

A: That's a personal question, but here's what I have in my bag as of this writing:

Driver (9.5 degree)
3-wood
3-hybrid
4-hybrid

5-iron
6-iron
7-iron
8-iron
9-iron
Pitching Wedge
Gap Wedge (52 degrees)
Sand Wedge (56 degrees)
Lob Wedge (60 degrees)
Putter

I have a hodge-podge mix of clubs and I still break 90 consistently. I have a Maxfli Driver that I love because I just seem to hit it so well. I actually broke it and found the same driver on eBay for just $30. It came with a matching 3-hybrid. I bought a used TaylorMade 3-wood at a second-hand store. Same with the Titleist 4-hybrid.

The irons (5-iron through gap wedge) are TaylorMade r7's I bought used from a friend for $100. The lob wedge is a Titleist Vokey I bought for $100 at my local course. I normally wouldn't pay that much for a club but I paid for it with the gift cards I won in my local weekend golf league. And the putter is a TaylorMade something or other I bought on sale at Golf Galaxy.

Club selection is a personal thing. All I'm saying is I don't believe you need to go out and spend a fortune on a new set of clubs to break 90. I'm living proof of that.
What's more important than the clubs is the person swinging them. And more importantly how that person swings them.

Buying a brand new $800 set of clubs is NOT going to make you a better golfer. Improving your fundamentals and your swing is going to make you a better golfer!

A Quick Word about Hybrid Clubs

Again, this is personal preference but I doubt anyone who can't break 90 should really have any iron longer than a 5-iron in the bag. So I'm advocating ditching the 3-iron and/or 4-iron in favor of a 3-hybrid and/or a 4-hybrid because they are much easier to hit.

You may even benefit from using a 5-hybrid instead of a 5-iron. I did it myself for a while. And if you prefer to swap out one of the hybrids for a 5-

wood, go for it.

Q: What is the best putter and what is the best grip?

A: Before we get into actually stroking putts. Let's talk about equipment – specifically about the best putters and the best grips. You'll hear this again but with few exceptions, I do not believe in any "one-size-fits-all" solutions. And that applies to putters too.

Some golfers are tall while others are short. Some have long arms. Others have big hands. We're all different. That's why I don't believe in preaching that a standard putter is better than a belly-putter or a long putter.

I don't believe a mallet putter is necessarily better than a blade putter. Or that an oversized grip is better than a standard grip. Or that a "claw-grip" is better than an overlapping grip when it comes to how you put your hands on the putter.

I believe you should use the equipment and the grip that feels best to YOU. I also believe you should verify this with results. For example, I've used the putting drills I'll share shortly to test different putters and different grips.

And based on the actual results, I've determined the best putter and grip for myself. I encourage you to do the same to determine the putter and grip the produces the best results for YOU!

Tracking Your Progress

In order to measure your improvement, you first need to assess your current skill level. You should know your handicap. If not, start tracking it today.

You also should know how far you hit each club. It could be a range. Here's what one source says. It sounds about right to me. The distances are broken down for men and women. The three numbers are for a short-hitter, an average hitter, and a long hitter.

In other words, for men a short hitter hits his drives 200 yards, an average length for the male driver is 230 yards, and if you can hit it 260 yards or more, you are considered a long hitter. These distances look about right to me.

Club	Men	Women
Driver	200-230-260	150-175-200
3-wood	180-215-235	125-150-180
5-wood	170-195-210	105-135-170
2-iron	170-195-210	105-135-170
3-iron	160-180-200	100-125-160
4-iron	150-170-185	90-120-150
5-iron	140-160-170	80-110-140
6-iron	130-150-160	70-100-130
7-iron	120-140-150	65-90-120
8-iron	110-130-140	60-80-110
9-iron	95-115-130	55-70-95
PW	80-105-120	50-60-80
SW	60-80-100	40-50-60

Q: What type of shafts should I use?

I'm NOT a club fitter. If you have questions I recommend you go see a professional club fitter. You can usually get some free advice from a place like Golf Galaxy or Golfsmith. They usually have driving cages in their stores where you can test out clubs and get your distances, club head speed, and many other statistics.

Ask the professional what shaft he recommends. There is extra stiff (X), stiff (S), regular (R), and senior (A). A because it originally called "amateur" flex.

As a general rule though, shaft flex is determined by club head speed. The faster your club head speed, the farther you hit the ball. So going by the distances above, short hitters should either use "A" shafts or even graphite shafts. Average hitters should use "R" shafts. Long hitters should use "S" shafts. And really long hitters might use "X" shafts.

Again, that's not written in stone it's just a general guideline. You might want to test different shafts and find the ones that are most comfortable to you. And the ones that help you hit the ball best – with both distance and accuracy.

Calibrate Your Distances

So your first task is to calibrate your distances. You should know how far you hit every club in your bag or a tight range. You can do this at any driving range. Most of them have yardage markers you can use to calibrate your distances.

It's a good idea to hit maybe 10 or 20 balls with each club. After hitting a dozen or two balls with the same club you should have a pretty good idea of the distance. You'll also want to do this two or three times on different days. You might feel looser or stronger one day and hit the ball farther.

Have your distances calibrated will give you more confidence on the golf course. For example, if you know you hit your 7-iron 140 – 150 yards, then you know exactly what club to pull out of your bag when you're 145 yards out. You can grab your 7-iron and take a confident swing.

And by calibrating your distances now, you'll really notice when you start hitting the ball farther as your fundamentals improve and your club head speed increases.

Believe me, it's a good day when you realize you need less club to hit the ball the same distance. Golf is a challenging game but it gets easier when you can hit your 7 or 8-iron 150 yards whereas you used to hit a 6 or 7-iron.

Week:
Date:

DISTANCE ASSESSMENT

Progress Check:
Measure Yardage for Every Club in Your Bag

Direction: At your practice facility, start with your lob wedge and work your way backwards until you are hitting your driver. Hit 6 practice balls with each (if possible, the balls you normally play, not range balls).

It's important to calibrate on a relatively windless day. I recommend using a rangefinder for this exercise. Mark each distance for each shot, then average by 6.

Clubs	1st Shot	2nd Shot	3rd Shot	4th Shot	5th Shot	6th Shot	AVG
LW							
SW							
GW							
PW							
9							
8							
7							
6							
5							
4							
3							
Hybrid 1							
Hybrid 2							
3-Wood							
Driver							

Copyright © Golf Aggressive LLP.

APPENDIX C: ANALYZING A ROUND OF GOLF

You may find it helpful to analyze each round of golf you play. Personally I find thinking through each round and writing down notes to be a great way to find the weaknesses in my game.

It could be something as simple as tracking the number of fairways and greens you hit and the number of putts for each hole. You can easily do this on your scorecard as you play.

And if you want to more elaborate you can create an Excel spreadsheet to track how well you are developing your critical golf skills. Here's an example I created.

Hole	Actual Par	Personal Par	My Score	Drive 200 yds + and in play	Approach shot near (or on) green	Chip or Pitch on Green	2-putt or Better	Holy Grail 3 into 2
1	4	5	5	YES	YES	YES	YES	NO
2	5	5	5	YES	YES	N/A (GIR)	YES	N/A (GIR)
3	4	4	4	YES	YES	N/A (GIR)	YES	N/A (GIR)
4	3	4	4	N/A (PAR 3)	YES	YES	YES	NO
5	4	5	4	YES	YES	N/A (GIR)	YES	N/A (GIR)
6	5	5	4	YES	YES	N/A (GIR)	YES	N/A (GIR)
7	4	4	4	YES	YES	N/A (GIR)	YES	N/A (GIR)
8	3	4	3	N/A (PAR 3)	YES	N/A (GIR)	YES	N/A (GIR)
9	4	5	7	NO	YES	N/A	NO	NO
Front Total	36	41	40					

Hole	Actual Par	Personal Par	My Score	Drive 200 yds + and in play	Approach shot near (or on) green	Chip or Pitch on Green	2-putt or Better	Holy Grail 3 into 2
10	3	4	4	N/A (PAR 3)	YES	YES	YES	NO
11	3	4	5	N/A (PAR 3)	YES	NO	YES	NO
12	4	5	5	YES	NO	YES	YES	YES
13	4	5	5	YES	YES	NO	YES	NO
14	4	5	5	YES	YES	NO	YES	NO
15	5	5	5	YES	YES	YES	YES	YES
16	4	4	3	YES	YES	N/A (GIR)	YES	YES
17	3	3	3	N/A (PAR 3)	YES	N/A (GIR)	YES	N/A (GIR)
18	4	5	5	NO	NO	YES	YES	NO
Back Total	34	40	40					
Total Score	70	81	80					

As you can see there are columns to track the actual par, my personal par, and my actual score for each hole. Then there are columns for each of the critical golf skills – tee shots, approach shots, chipping and pitching, and putting.

You may also find it helpful to color code the results as I have. Green means success and red means failure. It's easy to take a look and see where the red marks pile up. That tells you what skills you need to practice most.

Overall I'm fairly happy with this round – although I was quite disappointed at how a few mistakes prevented me from breaking 80.

You can see I only 3-putted one time. 11 of my 13 drives were hit at least 200+ yards and in play. I hit 16 of 18 approach shots on or near the green (that includes tee shots on par 3's). I hit 8 greens in regulation – nearly half! That's very good for me.

When I missed the green, I was able to pitch or chip the ball on to the green 6 of 9 times. That's a skill I need to work on in my quest to consistently break 80. And I even shaved 3 strokes of my score with the "holy grail" of golf – getting "up and down" from off the green and turning 3 shots into 2.

I only recall missing one short putt inside 5 feet that I fell like I should have made. However, I also remember leaving both an eagle putt and a birdie putt short of the hole. And to make matters worse, they were both right on line so I think with the proper speed they both would have gone into the hole!

From this it appears I need to get just a little bit better at each of the critical golf skills to reach a level where I'm consistently breaking 80. I've already broken 80 several times with a personal best of 77.

If you'll commit yourself to the regular practice that will improve your golf skills, you'll be rewarded with scores that continue to drop. First you'll start consistently breaking 90, then your scores will drop even more as you keep practicing and keep improving your critical golf skills.

And to prove skill matters more than equipment, I'll tell you that I was traveling without my own clubs so I played this particular round with borrowed clubs I had never hit before and I played in my sneakers too.

If you're really serious, you could write yourself a brief synopsis of how you played each hole, what you were thinking on each shot, and how you selected the club you used. If you're like most golfers, you remember every shot on every hole – especially if you've played the course several times.

This can take a little time and you should do it soon after your round. Like me, you may find this exercise helpful in identifying mental mistakes that cost you strokes. I wrote a few pages about my recent round. You can read it as an example. Plus you can see how I thought one shot ahead on several occasions to save myself valuable strokes.

Here's the scorecard. We played from the blue tees which was appropriate since my friend and I are both about 12 handicaps. If you were a higher handicapper that can't consistently break 90, you'd probably want to play this course from the white tees.

BLUE TEES	390	475	376	178	340	466	329	198	392	3144	BLUE	197	223	342	380	345	470	295	127	320	2699	5843
WHITE TEES	375	465	366	168	325	456	318	183	377	3033	WHITE	188	213	336	370	334	461	280	116	311	2609	5642
PAR	4	5	4	3	4	5	4	3	4	36	PAR	3	3	4	4	4	5	4	3	4	34	70
HANDICAP	1	3	7	17	9	13	11	15	5		HANDICAP	12	10	6	4	8	2	16	18	14		

						WE																
HOLE NUMBER	1	2	3	4	5	6	7	8	9	OUT	HOLE	10	11	12	13	14	15	16	17	18	IN	TOT	HCP	NET
						THEY																

PACE OF PLAY	:14	:15	:14	:13	:14	:15	:14	:14	:15	2:08	PACE	:15	:14	:14	:14	:14	:15	:14	:13	:14	2:07	4:15
HANDICAP	13	3	11	17	7	5	9	15	1		HANDICAP	12	16	4	6	8	2	14	18	10		
PAR	5	5	4	3	4	5	4	3	4	37	PAR	3	4	4	4	4	5	4	3	4	35	72
RED TEES	360	454	287	157	310	445	307	168	362	2850	RED	158	203	320	337	322	355	218	104	301	2318	5168

Warm-up: I ALWAYS do some type of warm-up even if it's just stretching. This course does not have a driving range so I didn't have a chance to hit these clubs at all. The first time I hit any of them was on the course. However I did spend a few minutes on the putting green and also hit a few chip shots just to get a feel for the greens.

1st Hole

This is a straight hole with woods on the left. So you don't want to go left or you could be out of bounds. There's plenty of room to the right. You can even play from the 7th fairway if you go way right. I know this because I've done it before. This hole was also playing into a decent breeze.

Bottom Line: Do NOT hook your tee shot into the woods.

Tee shot: Driver. I pulled the driver out of the bag and teed it up. I immediately noticed the tee I was using was short but I hit the ball of it anyway. It was a decent shot. I started a bit right and drew slightly back into the middle of the fairway.

2nd shot: I was about 180 yards out so my drive only went 210 yards. That's A LOT shorter than usual. Apparently the combination of the low tee and the wind in my face led to a short tee shot. Oh well, it went 200+ yards and it's in play. Good enough.

I chose a 6-iron which is my normal 180-yard club even though the wind was in my face. I did this because the last time I played I was consistently hitting shots over the green and because long is bad on this hole – especially considering the pin was deep. So an approach shot over the green would have left me short sided.

So I played smart and hit one less club knowing that if I struck it well it could reach the green but at worst I would be up near the green where I could chip the ball onto the green. I struck it well but pulled it a bit left and ended up in the bunker about pin high.

3rd shot: I'm not a great bunker player – not even a good bunker player really. So I just wanted to get the ball onto the green, 2-putt for bogey and walk to the second tee. I did manage to hit my bunker shot on to the green leaving myself about a 15-foot putt. Not bad.

4th shot: I read this putt to break a bit right but it didn't break as much as I read. Reading too much break seems to be pretty common among mid to high-handicap golfers so be careful of this. In any event, my speed was very good. The putt rolled past the hole about 6-inches leaving a tap-in

5th shot: Tap in.

2nd Hole

This one is a short par 5 with a huge dog leg right – about 90 degrees. You can either try to hit the tee shot over some trees to make the hole even shorter. Or you can just knock it out past the dog leg and leave yourself a longer second shot.

Tee shot: I hit driver again but this time I borrowed some longer tees from my playing partner. I never saw my tee shot (because I keep my head down and don't peek!). However, my playing partner saw it in the air and I saw it land just past the dog leg leaving me a long second shot to the green.

2nd shot: I had about 220 yards to the green so this drive went 255 yards – much better. Apparently teeing the ball up a bit higher made a big difference. I figured I might need a 3-wood to reach the green – especially considering it was a cool Spring day meaning the ball wouldn't go as far.

However, this was a blind shot and I knew that long on this hole is not good. There is water not far past the hole so you don't want to go long. And there are greenside bunkers to both the left and the right. So being a bit short of the green is the safe shot leaving a short chip.

So again, I used a little less club. Instead of 3-wood I pulled a 5-wood. I hit it well but it drifted left again – most of my shots go a bit left. I couldn't see where the shot ended up and I was a bit concerned as we rode up but we found the ball in the left rough about 20 yards short of the green leaving an easy chip.

3rd shot: I struck a sold chip that landed on the green and was right on line. The ball came to a stop about 5 feet short of the hole leaving a very makeable birdie putt.

4th shot: I read this putt to break slightly right but again it didn't quite break as much as I read so I missed it left. Fortunately the speed was good again leaving me about 18 inches past the hole so I tapped in for an easy – if not disappointing – par.

5th shot: Tap-in

3rd Hole

This is a fairly straight and short par 4 but it's uphill so it plays a bit longer than it appears. Out-of-bounds left and tall weeds right but the landing area is generous so just don't yank the tee shot too far left and you should be fine.

Tee shot: I ripped the tee shot down the right side and it drew back into the fairway.

2nd shot: I was about 100 yards out so this drive was 265 – getting better. This shot was both uphill and into a bit of a breeze and I played a sand wedge. That's my normal 100-yard club but I've always felt more comfortable taking an aggressive swing with less club than trying to take less than a full swing with more club. Plus the pin was red – meaning towards the front of the green.

There is out of bounds and sand left so you don't want to go there. That being the case I consciously "held off" on my swing. That just means I tried not to let the club release like normal. I did this because my tendency is to draw the ball and as I said you don't want to go left on this hole.

The technique worked because my ball actually ended up right of a pin on the right side of the green. I was about pin high but maybe 20 feet with a big breaking side hill putt.

3rd shot: Well, at least I had the line right. Unfortunately my speed was not so good. Not only did I not get this putt to the hole, it wasn't even inside my "circle of confidence." I had about 5 feet and it was still a side hill putt that broke left.

4th shot: Drained it! Thank goodness it hit the hole because it had plenty of speed. That's the benefit of having confidence on the greens though – you can stroke putts confidently and aggressively and you'll make more of them!

4th Hole

This is a medium length par 3 of 178 yards but it's downhill so it doesn't play quite as long as you think. Plus the wind was helping a bit. Long is not good plus the green is guarded by bunkers. But the green is quite large so you ought to be able to hit it.

Tee shot: 6-iron is my normal 180 club but as I said this hole was playing a bit down wind and also down hill so I went down a club to a 7-iron. I wasn't certain this was enough club but short is better than long. Even if I were to be short I would leave myself with a simple pitch. That was the plan at least.

I crushed the tee shot plus it had a decent draw on it and that makes it fly even farther. The ball landed about pin-high but left of the green and on a downslope. I lost of sight of it as it bounced down a hill but I knew there were tall weeds down there so I feared I had hit it out-of-bounds.

Fortunately I stayed just left of the big weeds and I was safe. But I was also short sided with an uphill pitch to a green sloping away from me. Not good.

2nd shot: My thought here was just to get the ball onto the green and 2-putt for bogey. I used a 50-degree wedge. If I'd had my clubs I'd have used a 60-degree wedge but all I had was the 50 so that's what I used.

I struck a decent pitch that ended up about 15 feet past the hole. Not too bad. I ought to be able to 2-putt from 15 feet and maybe even sink the putt.

3rd shot: This may sound repetitive but again I rolled a putt with good speed that didn't break quite as much as I saw – at least not until after it passed the hole. In any event, I left myself a tap in for bogey.

4th shot: Tap-in.

5th Hole

This hole doesn't look difficult but it can be. There's a fence down the left side and anything over the fence is out of bounds. There's water on the right so you could end up wet if you go too far right. And there's a big bunker in the middle of the fairway about 240 yards out.

Tee shot: My playing partner hit driver and he hit a good one. However, the smart play is to layup short of the fairway bunker leaving yourself a short approach shot. So I hit my 5-wood off the tee and just as planned ended up short of the fairway bunker.

2nd shot: I was about 110 yards out so my tee shot went about 230 yards. This is a fairly large green but there's still the fence on the left so anything over there is out of bounds. There's more trouble long and there's a big bunker in front of the green.

So the safe shot is to the right and that was the target I chose with my sand wedge. I "held off" again just as I had down on the 3rd hole and it worked again. I ended up with a long putt from the right side of the green. And if I had missed the green I'd have had an easy chip.

3rd shot: I read this putt perfectly and it was headed straight into the cup – until it stopped about three feet short. Frustrating! But you don't expect to make many 30 foot putts so I can't be too disappointed.

4th shot: I made the 3-foot par putt.

6th Hole

This is a short par 5 with a big dog leg left. However, it can be dangerous to try to cut too much off this hole. There's a fence down the left side that's out of bounds and lots of tall grass and weeds before you get to the fence that can eat up your ball. There's plenty of room right but that leaves you with a longer second shot.

Tee shot: I picked a spot (a specific tree) I thought would be a good aiming point and hit my driver hard expecting my normal draw. Of course, this one didn't draw. It actually faded slightly. I went through the fairway and ended up under a tree.

2nd shot: I actually wasn't in a bad spot. I had a decent lie where I could take a full swing without hitting the tree and I had a good angle to the green. That being the case I pulled my 3-wood out of the bag for this 220-yard uphill shot.

I've hit so many 3-woods both at the driving range and on the course that I'm confident I can give it a whack – even if it's not my club! And whack it I did. I actually ended up on the green with about a 20-foot eagle putt.

3rd shot: The good news is I read the putt perfectly – a slight break to the right. The bad news is I left it about 12-inches short. Bummer! I've only had 3 or 4 eagles in my life so another one would have been nice. But there's nothing wrong with a tap in birdie.

4th shot: Tap in.

7th Hole

This is a fairly short par 4 with a slight dog leg left.

Tee shot: I hammered a driver with a slight draw to about 50 yards from the green. That's roughly a 280-yard drive.

2nd shot: This was actually an awkward distance. I prefer to be a bit further back. I'm confident with a sand wedge from 100 yards. So in hindsight perhaps I should have hit less club to leave myself at a more favorable distance. This involved some guesswork.

I grabbed the 50-degree wedge and struck it solidly without about a half swing. Fortunately I guessed right. It headed straight for the pin, landed on the green and left me about a 15-foot birdie putt.

3rd shot: A familiar story. The speed was good. The ball rolled just past the hole but again it didn't break quite as much as I thought. I tapped in for par.

4th shot: Tap-in

8th Hole

This was a longish par 3 – about 200 yards to a back pin. Considering the back pin, hitting the tee shot over the green would leave you short-sided and there's a bunker to the right. So in this case it's better to be short than long.

Tee shot: I hit a 5-iron. It may not have been quite enough club but I knew if I struck it well I could get it at least to the green. However, I'm not overly confident with my own 4-iron let alone someone else's! So I stuck with the 5-iron. I hit it slightly "fat" – I hit the ground behind the ball just a tad before I hit the ball. However, the ball land short of the green and rolled forward onto the green leaving me with a long birdie putt.

2nd shot: This must have been a 60-footer. It was so long I lost sight of my marker as I was lining up my putt from behind the hole. This was not a good putt. I left it 5 feet short – outside my "circle of confidence."

3rd shot: Fortunately I left myself a fairly straight putt and it rolled into the right side of the cup for par.

9th hole

This is a challenging hole with a dogleg right. There's a tree line down the left side and that's out of bounds. And there are tall trees on the right too. It leaves a narrow opening for your tee shot.

Tee shot: I pulled out my driver – and promptly shanked it dead right into some trees that shouldn't even be in play on this hole. I have no idea why. I had been hitting ball well all day and I felt confident over the ball. I must have hit it off the toe or something. Or maybe it was my mind. I had a great round going. I was only one stroke over par up to this point and I was thinking about going low. Maybe that was it. Who knows?

2nd shot: Penalty stroke!

3rd shot: So here I am – still on the tee box – hitting my third shot. What a bummer! And there's not much worse in golf than teeing it up and staring down a narrow fairway after you've just shanked the same shot about 30 seconds ago!

I took what I swear was the same swing and I crushed it over the trees on the right and watched it draw back into the fairway. Oh well, shake it off and move on I guess.

4th shot: I was about 110 yards out so this drive – well 2nd drive and 3rd shot – but whatever it was I hit it about 280 yards. I hit a sand wedge and pulled it a bit left. It landed on the other side of a sand trap and bounced forward. It ended up on the back of the green leaving a long double-breaker putt. Fantastic!!

5th shot: I think I read the putt fairly well but I'll never know for sure because I left it so short!! I had about a 6 or 8 foot putt for double bogey!!

6th shot: I got the putt to the hole but missed right and tapped in for a 7!! Nice job. Way to ruin a great front nine!

7th shot: tap-in for triple bogey!

10th Hole

This is longish par 3 of just under 200 yards. It's a similar distance to the 8th hole so I considered using the same club off the tee – a 5-iron. However, there are other factors to consider here.

First, this hole plays a bit downhill so I may want to use less club. Second, and more importantly, this green is surrounded by trouble everywhere but short. If your tee shot is long, you're in the woods. If your tee shot is more than say 10 yards left or right, you're also in the woods.

Yet if your tee shot is a bit short you'll be left with simple chip shot to a green that slopes from the back down to the front. The smart play is obvious so I kept the 5-iron in the bag and pulled the 6-iron.

A well-struck 6-iron may get to the green and I know I can't hit it over the green so I'm taking long out of play. I'm also more confident I can hit a 6-iron fairly straight than I am with a 5-iron so that's another good reason to hit the tee shot with one less club.

The most likely outcome is that I'll be short and leave myself an easy chip to the green. That's fine because my personal par on this hole is 4. All I need to do is chip the ball on to the green and 2-putt.

Tee Shot: As expected I struck a solid 6-iron that drew a bit to the left. It ended up maybe 10 yards short of the green leaving me an easy chip shot to a back pin.

2nd shot: I hit a pretty mediocre chip shot that I pulled left of my target. Yet I still put the ball on the green so now all I had to do was 2-putt for my personal par.

3rd shot: My mediocre chip left me with about a 15-foot side hill putt with a big left to right break. I stroked a bad putt. I left the putt about 5 feet short so not inside my "circle of confidence."

4th shot: Thankfully I drained the putt. All the time I've devoted to putting is paying off today. I've only missed one putt from within 5 feet.

11th Hole

This is another challenging par 3. It plays about 225 yards with a huge drop in elevation. There are trees long and there's not much room to the right of the green either. There's plenty of room to the left of the green and short. The problem is that if you miss the green, you'll have a challenging pitch shot to an elevated green.

On a warm summer day I might hit a 5-iron or my 3-hybrid. However, this was a cool spring day so the ball wasn't going as far and remember I played this round with borrowed clubs. I decided to use the 5-wood because I had already struck it well several times.

Tee shot: The tee shot was well struck and came to rest pin-high. Unfortunately I hit a big hook. When I really go after a shot as I did on this one, I tend to get "quick" and that's exactly what happened here.

The clubface was closed at impact which put a right to left side spin on the ball. It started out at the center of the green yet as the force of the initial strike on the ball wore off the sidespin took over and produced a sizable hook. The ball came to rest roughly pin-high about 20 yards left of the green.

2nd shot: My tee shot left me with a challenging pitch shot. Not only that, since the pin was on the left side of the green I was also short-sided. My goal was just to pitch the ball on to the green and 2-putt for my personal par.

However, I struck the ball a bit fat and ended up a few yards short of the green, just off the fringe, and still in the rough. What a bad mistake! Now I left myself with an even harder shot.

In hindsight, I'll remember two things for the next time I find myself in a position like this. First, just get the ball on the green! I should have pretended the flag stick was on the right-hand side of the green and just pitched it on the green. Even if I was way long, I'd still leave myself with a putt.

And secondly, I needed to swing just a bit harder. My club head got caught up in the thick rough. That slowed down my club head speed just enough that I came up short. You need to swing a bit more aggressively to hit the ball out of heavy rough.

3rd shot: I chipped the ball on to the green but not close. I was short-sided and I didn't want to get too cute and leave it short again! Or "skull" a shot over the green.

4th shot: I lagged a 20 foot putt inside my "circle of confidence" and tapped in for a disappointing double-bogey 5.

5th shot: Tap-in.

12th Hole

For me, this is one of the most challenging holes on the course. It's a short par 4, however, it requires you to hit accurate shots. It's got about a 45 degree dogleg right and there's a creek about 220 yards out. So most golfers will hit less than driver off this tee box. Second, the fairway narrows considerably past the creek and there are tall trees both left and right.

To put yourself in good position for your 2nd shot, you need to hit a drive of about 200-yards and preferably down the left side of the fairway to give yourself a good angle. You may be blocked off from the green if you're not far enough left.

Tee shot: I struck a sold 5-iron off this tee. It started down the left side of the fairway and drew a bit more left.

2nd shot: My tee shot ended up in the left rough leaving me a clear shot to a small green about 140 yards out. I chose an 8-iron and did not strike it well. The rough closed my club head and I ended up pulling the shot into the woods on the left – out of bounds! This hole always seems to give me trouble.

3rd shot: I found my ball in the woods, assessed myself a penalty stroke, and took a drop.

4th shot: I had short chip shot of about 30-yards which played quite well. The golf ball came to a stop pin-high and about 5 feet right of the flag.

5th shot: I drained the putt. My short game saved me on this hole. I pulled off the "holy grail" for golfers by turning 3 shots into 2. And by doing so, I scored my personal par on this hole despite the penalty stroke.

13th Hole

This is a fairly short par 4 with a slight dog leg right. The tee is elevated and there are trees down the left hand side. Anything left is out of bounds. There are also trees down the right side but they just separate the 13th and 14th fairways so right is much better than left. You'll probably find your ball if you hit it right and you may even have clear shot at the green – or you may be stuck behind a tree.

Tee shot: Considering several factors, I left the driver in the bag and hit 3-wood off this tee. It's a short par 4 that plays even shorter because the tees are elevated so 3-wood is plenty of club for me. Plus my naturally tendency is to draw the ball to the left and left is out of bounds on this hole.

I struck my 3-wood solidly and started it down the tree line on the right expecting it to draw back into the fairway. However, this time my tee shot didn't draw. We didn't see it land be we know it was somewhere in the tree line – or so we thought.

2nd shot: We couldn't find my tee shot. Then the group in front of us pointed it out. Apparently it had hit a tree and bounced right – into the 14th fairway. Actually not a bad break because I was in a fairway – not my fairway – but a fairway nonetheless so I had a good lie. And I also had a shot at the green. There was a tall tree blocking the front of the green that required a bit of a draw but that's my natural shot so that's fine with me.

I grabbed my 5-wood and put a confident stroke on the ball striking it solidly. The shot did draw to the left. However, it drew too soon and/or too much and headed straight for the big tree blocking the green. Fortunately the ball didn't strike any branches solidly and sailed though the tree coming to rest about 20 yards short of the green.

3rd shot: This was not a particularly difficult chip shot. I had plenty of green to work with. However I was a bit too aggressive and the ball went over the green and barely into the rough on the other side of the green. This is a reminder that I need to work on my "touch" and "feel" around the greens.

4th shot: Technically this was another chip shot. However since the ball was barely in the rough and I was short-sided I elected to use my putter. I'm more comfortable keeping the ball as close to the ground as possible so I putt whenever I can. My putt/chip rolled about 5 feet past the hole leaving me a "tester" for my personal par.

5th shot: This was a left-edge putt that would break to the right. I stroked the putt with just enough speed to reach the hole and it fell into the "side door" for my personal par. Again, my putting saved the day – or at least the hole.

14th Hole

This is not a particularly long par 4 and the fairway is plenty wide to bomb a driver out there. The only danger is the street on the left that's out of bounds. The challenge on this hole is that the green is very elevated – probably 50 feet or more from the right side. And not only that, the green is small and slopes steeply from left to right.

Tee shot: I hit a solid drive that left me in perfect position – about 110 yards out and in the fairway. So this was a drive of roughly 270 yards.

2nd shot: I chose my sand wedge for the approach shot and struck it reasonably well. It landed on the green. However, the ball landed a bit too far on the right side of the green so it rolled off the green and barely into the rough leaving me a difficult shot.

3rd shot: This was difficult position. The ball was in thick rough but only a few inches off the fringe. Plus there's wasn't much green to work with and the green sloped away from me. I decided to use my putter which may or may not have been a bad decision, however I did not strike the ball solidly and the ball didn't even make the green. It came to a stop on the fringe. Perhaps I should have used a wedge.

4th shot: I putted this shot from the fringe and safely into my "circle of confidence" from about 15 feet. Then tapped in for my personal par.

5th shot: Tap-in.

Just out of curiosity I tried my 3rd shot one more time again using the putter. This time I struck the ball more solidly and put the ball inside my "circle of confidence." Frankly I'll strive to not leave myself in this difficult situation again. Just hit your approach shot on the green!

15th Hole

This is a short par 5. It's a bit odd though in that the tee is elevated and you can't see the green from the tee box. Your tee shot goes into a valley. Then the terrain rises and falls again so there's a second valley on this hole and a very elevated green that's also quite small.

Tee shot: I hit a sold drive down the right side but it failed to draw back into the fairway so I left myself in the right rough. However I still had a decent lie and a straight shot to the green even though it was a blind shot. I was about 220 yards out so my drive went about 250 yards.

2nd shot: We had to wait on the group in front of us so we drove up where I could pick a spot to aim my blind approach shot. I was close enough that I could reach the green with a solid 3-wood and there really isn't any trouble so why not go for it?

I hit a lousy 3-wood that ended up on the top of the hill about 130-yards out. Not bad for a crappy shot!

3rd shot: This was a fairly straight forward shot except that the ball was below my feet which tends to make the ball go right. I'm not sure exactly what happened but I made terrible contact with the ball and hit a low line-drive to the right. Frankly it reminded me of the past when I was a really lousy iron player and I'd just "slap" the ball up towards the green and let my short game take over.

4th shot: After two really mediocre shots I was just off the green and had plenty of green to work with. If I could get "up and down" I could still save par. I struck a pretty good chip shot that broke to the left and ended up about 5 feet below the hole.

5th shot: I sunk the 5 foot par putt. For the second time, I turned 3 shots into 2 and saved my personal par – which on this hole was the real par – a 5.

16th Hole

This is a short, straight par 4. I've actually reached the green on this hole off the tee. The only trouble is out of bounds left but it's way left and there's plenty of room to the right so it's a green light special. I pulled out my driver.

Tee shot: I hit the tee shot I had imagined. It started down the right side and draw back to the left. On this cool, spring day the ball wasn't going as far as it will when the weather warms up so I was just short of the green – about 20 yards short. So this was a solid 275-yard drive.

2nd shot: This was a simple chip shot. The pin was in the back of the green leaving my plenty of room to work with. My distance was good but I pulled the chip a bit left leaving me pin high and about 20 feet to the left of the cup.

3rd shot: To my eye this looked like a putt that would break slightly to the right. I stroked it and watched it roll toward the cup. It looked pretty good – and it fell into the hole for a birdie!! For the second hole in row I had pulled off the "holy grail" for golfers – turning 3 shots into 2. Last hole it save par, this hole it gave me a birdie.

17th Hole

According to the scorecard this is the easiest hole on the course and I don't disagree. It's a short par 3 to an elevated green. The card says it's 127 yards to the middle of the green. Today the pin was on the front part of the green and the breeze was helping a bit. So I figured the shot would play about 110 to 115 yards.

Tee shot: Sand wedge was my club of choice and I struck it well favoring the right side because while the terrain to the right of the green is level there's a big drop off to the left so you don't want to be there. The ball landed on the green about pin high and left me about a 20 foot birdie putt.

2nd shot: This putt was a bit downhill and broke a bit right to left. I struck with good speed but it broke more than I expected as it lost speed. The ball made it to the hole but I missed it on the low side. No problem. You don't expect to make many 20 foot putts. I left it well within my "circle of confidence" and tapped in for par.

3rd shot: Tap-in for par. Back to back 3's are a great way to lower your score!

18th Hole

This is a straight par 4. It's not particularly long and while there's out of bounds on the left and right, there's plenty of room to land your tee shot. The challenge is the green. It slopes severely from back to front leaving some hellacious putts from certain spots.

Tee shot: I chose driver and easily hit my 2nd worst drive off the day. I'm not sure what went wrong but my tendency is to get quick and hit a hook when I try to kill the ball and I suspect that's what happened here.

Fortunately I also hit it low so the rough grabbed it and it also appeared bounce off something and back into the left rough. I maybe gotten a lucky break that turned an out of bounds tee shot into just a woefully pathetic tee shot that was still in play. It certainly did not go 200 yards so I failed in my goal hit the tee shot at least 200 yards but I did keep it in play.

2nd shot: The ball was in thick rough and under some trees too so I need to keep this shot low. In an effort to hit a low shot, I positioned the ball a bit further back in my stance. I wasn't trying to play a "hero" shot. All I wanted to do was to advance the ball up toward the green where I could chip it on and two-putt at worst.

It was not to be. I hit another terrible shot. It was low alright but it had a draw and got stuck in the left rough again. I doubt it went more than 60 yards. I was still 100 yards out! So on this short 320-yard par 4 hole, I had barely hit my first two shots 200 yards. Pathetic!!

3rd shot: Fortunately I had no obstacles – like trees – to overcome this time. Just a clear shot to the green. My sand wedge had good distance but this shot was pulled a tad left so I had about a 30-foot side hill putt with a big break from left to right.

4th shot: This is the type of putt you just want to "lag" into your "circle of confidence" and tap in for a 2-putt. My putt rolled past the hole and safely into the back half of my "COC" where I tapped in for a bogey 5 – my personal par.

5th shot: Tap-in.

End of Journal.

You don't have to write a short novel like I just did, yet I find it extremely helpful to think through my round and I gain even more insights if I take the time to put my thoughts into writing.

You can see how I used the critical golf skills I've shared to help me easily break 90 – and just one shot away from shooting a score in the 70s. Let's review the 6 critical golf skills and see how they applied to this round of golf.

Critical Golf Skill #1: Consistently 2-putt most greens (Minimize three-putts)

I 3-putted once – on the 9th hole. That's because I've developed the skill to "lag" long putts into my "circle of confidence" and then make the putts inside my "COC." I've done this by practicing the same drills I've shared with you.

Critical Golf Skill #2: When you miss the green in regulation, pitch or chip the golf ball onto the green (the first time – and of course the nearer the hole the better!)

I missed 10 greens in regulation and 7 of those 10 times I was able to get the ball on the green and 2-putt. That's not bad yet I'm striving to increase that to 10 out of 10. That's how you save precious strokes and lower your scores.

Critical Golf Skill #3: Turn 3 shots into 2 (Get "up and down" like a PGA pro!)

3 times I was able to turn 3 shots into 2. That's 3 strokes shaved off my score. One more and I would have broken 80. This is the reason to practice your short game. The closer you can chip and pitch the ball to the hole and the more times you drain the putt, the faster you'll lower your scores.

Critical Golf Skill #4: Consistently hit your tee shots 200 yards or more AND keep them in play! (300-yard drives into the woods won't help you lower your scores.)

With the exception of the inexplicable shank on the 9th hole and the terrible tee shot on 18, I consistently hit my drives 250+ and not just in play, in the fairway most of the time. I can get better but getting off the tee hasn't been my biggest obstacle to lowering my scores.

Critical Golf Skill #5: Consistently hit approach shots near the green (on the green is even better) and eliminate "mis-hits" like "fat" shots and "thin" shots.

7 out of 18 greens in regulation – almost half. This is a big improvement that has allowed me to lower my scores. Eliminating "mis-hits" is an area where I've improved a great deal and it's a big reason why my scores have dropped to 80 and below. These days most of my "mis-hits" even end up near the green.

Critical Golf Skill #6: Keep the big numbers off the card (Play Smart Golf!)

7 was my biggest number this entire round. Not long ago, it was not unusual for me to have multiple 7's and 8's in the same round. I've developed the skill to play smart and minimize the damage.

Consider how many times I played one shot ahead and hit one less club just to keep myself out of trouble – and the big numbers that often come with trouble.

The quickest way to lower your scores is to develop these 6 critical golf skills. Keep practicing and improving and I'm confident you'll be consistently breaking 90 faster than you ever imagined.

APPENDIX D: ASSESSMENT SHEETS

Use the following sheets to track your progress through the 6 Critical Golf Skills. Measuring your progress on the practice of golf will help you find weakness and strengths in your game.

Once you have created a baseline for each critical golf skill, your task is to try and beat your benchmark scores each week. Remember, we are looking to improve each week until you are breaking 90 at the end of the 42 days.

If you would like downloadable and printable versions of all of the Assessment Sheets, please visit the following URL and enter your name:

http://golff.it/9042

You will also receive bonus video's as well as future mailing from the How to Break 90 in 42 Days or Less team.

ROBERT PHILLIPS

CRITICAL GOLF
SKILL #1

Week:
Date:

PUTTING ASSESSMENT

Progress Check: 3-Foot Putts (Circle of Confidence)

Direction: Place 5 balls around a relatively flat hole. Stroke each putt and repeat process 4 more times, for a total of 25 putts. If you miss a putt, keep going until you have stroked 25 putts total.

RESULTS
Total Putts Made: ____

Pressure Test: Streak Tracker

Direction: Track how many 3' putts you make in a row and compete to beat your score each week.

RESULTS
Streak (made in a row): ____

Progress Check: 15' Lag Putts into Circle of Confidence

Direction: Stroke 25 putts to within 3' around your target hole. Track how many make it into the Circle of Confidence and mark the point each ball stops.

RESULTS
Total within Circle of Confidence: ____

Pressure Test: Holing Out

Direction: On ALL lag putts, stroke the second putt and track your two-putts.

RESULTS
Total Two-Putts: ____

Copyright © Golf Aggressive LLP.

HOW TO BREAK 90 IN 42 DAYS OR LESS

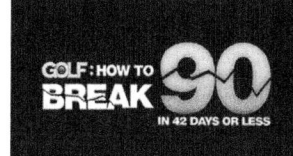 

CRITICAL GOLF
SKILL #2

Week:
Date:

CHIPPING ASSESSMENT

Progress Check: Assess Chipping to Close, Medium, and Far Pin

Direction: Take 25 chip shots each to a close, middle, and far pin placements. Your goal is to leave them inside a 15 foot circle surrounding the hole.

CLOSE PIN
(10 Balls)

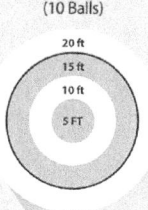

MIDDLE PIN
(10 Balls)

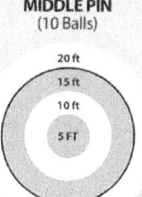

FAR PIN
(10 Balls)

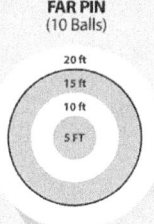

RESULTS	RESULTS	RESULTS
Inside 15 feet: ____	Inside 15 feet: ____	Inside 15 feet: ____

Pressure Test: Holing Out

Direction: Putt out the chips. Keep track of how many times you get "up and down" and how many times you 2-putt.

RESULTS
Up and Downs: ____
2-Putts: ____

Copyright © Golf Aggressive LLP.

HOW TO BREAK 90 IN 42 DAYS OR LESS

TEE SHOT ASSESSMENT

Progress Check:
200+ Yard Tee Shot AND Land in Fairway

Direction: Take 25 tee shots and keep track of how many you hit at least 200 yards AND keep in play.

TEE SHOT RESULTS

200 Yards or Longer: ____

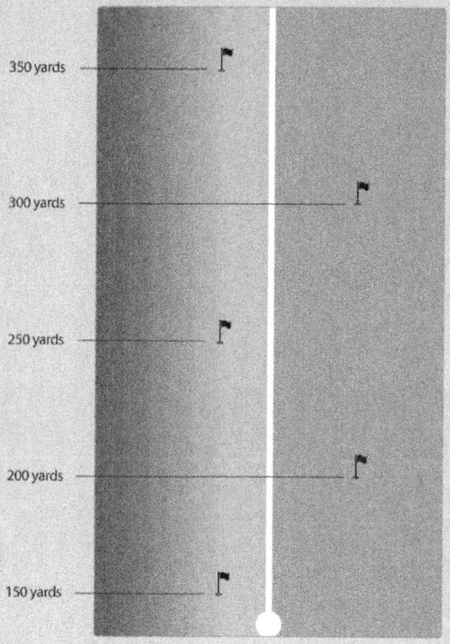

Pressure Test:
Keep it in the Fairway

Direction: In addition to tracking yardage, track if your ball landed in the fairway or rough. You should also plot the side of the fairway the ball lands on, as this is useful information to show shot patterns.

RESULTS

200+ Yards AND in Fairway: ____

Copyright © Golf Aggressive LLP.

ROBERT PHILLIPS

HOW TO BREAK 90 IN 42 DAYS OR LESS

CRITICAL GOLF
SKILL #4

Week:
Date:

100-YARD APPROACH SHOTS

Progress Check:
Assess 100-Yard Approach Shots

Direction: Hit 25 iron shots to a target 100-yards away. Keep track of how many hit the green (or would have hit the green if you don't have a green to shoot for).

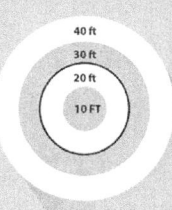

100-YARD APPROACH RESULTS

Hit Green: _____

Pressure Test: Pin Seeker

Direction: Track how many shots land within 20' of the pin.

RESULTS

Inside 20': _____

Copyright © Golf Aggressive LLP

CRITICAL GOLF SKILL #5

Week:
Date:

HITTING 150-YARD IRON SHOTS ON (OR NEAR) THE GREEN

Progress Check: Assess 150-Yard Approach Shots

Direction: Hit 25 iron shots to a target 150-yards away. Keep track of how many hit the green (or would have hit the green if you don't have a green to shoot for).

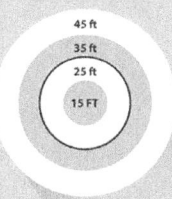

150-YARD APPROACH RESULTS

Hit Green: _____

Pressure Test: Pin Seeker

Direction: Track how many shots land within 25' of the pin.

RESULTS

Inside 25': _____

Copyright © Golf Aggressive LLP.

ROBERT PHILLIPS

APPENDIX E: PRE-SHOT ROUTINE FORMULA

The pre-shot routine is THE PRIMARY KEY to lowering your score quickly... not in a month's time, but almost overnight.

The number of strokes you can shave off each round depends on how well your pre-shot routine is crafted. My sincere hope is that by the end of this chapter, you will have the basic knowledge to design a routine that fits your personal quirks and comfort level.

It's certainly not out of the realm of possibility to shave off 4 to 5 strokes per round once you have formed a good foundation.

The real secret to lowering your score comes by improving consistency... by doing the exact same things over and over and over again.

Sounds boring I know, but let's take a look at how computers work for some insight...

Why is a computer able to repeat the same task over and over again and always get the same result?

Because a computer follows the same exact routine for the task it is asked to perform. CONSISTENCY.

However, the computer is only as good as it's programmer. Programmed to follow the wrong formula or steps and the computer will deliver the wrong result. Programmed in the right manner, and the computer ALWAYS delivers the right answer.

As humans, it is impossible to meet the efficiency of a computer. Yet, we can get close to computer efficiency by developing routines aimed at solving different challenges golf provides. This may require more than one pre-shot routine based on the situation we are faced with.

For example, your putting routine will be different than your chipping routine or your driver routine. We must factor in different elements based on the problems presented to us to deliver satisfactory results.

Golfers at the top of their game like Rory and Tiger are able to replicate consistent results on a consistent basis – only because they have forged effective pre-shot routines based on different situations.

When Tiger or Rory are faced with a problematic situation, their programming kicks in and they react almost instinctively. This comes through practice and situation awareness – good programming.

For this article, I partnered with my good friend Richard Guzzo in order to help you craft a well designed Pre-Shot Routine. Richard also happens to be a highly decorated former collegiate golfer and the reigning club champion at The Hyatt Hill Country Resort in San Antonio, TX.

For a bit of background on how we stumbled upon our formula, I need to tell you how we arrived at putting this Pre-Shot Routine together.

In a recent survey to our GolfAggressive.com clients, Rich and I asked golfers to tell us their **number 1 biggest problem** when it comes to their golf games.

As the results came in, we started to see a lot of similarities. Almost every golfer mentioned consistency as their biggest issue. Hundreds of golfers all mentioned problems related to blow up holes, three putts, and all kinds of consistency issues.

Not surprising.

To be honest, the first step in improving consistency STARTS with a solid pre-shot routine. When I play with high-handicappers, I notice one INCONSISTENCY among them… they rarely follow the same pre-shot routine.

Being inconsistent here is killing their golf scores and letting those blow up holes slip into their rounds.

And it's important to know that no two golfers will perform their pre-shot routines the same. The goal here is to make your routine unique to you and one that makes you feel comfortable and confident over the ball.

Setting up the same way every time will deliver the consistency you desire.

And as mentioned, you should craft separate routines for putting, chipping, your driver, trouble shots, and sand shots to name just a few. The overall mechanics will be the same, but you will need to build in the different setups into your routines.

There are other ways to design consistency into our golf games, but the cornerstone of your game needs to be founded upon following the same steps for every shot you execute.

Take a look at the best free throw shooters in the NBA. They bounce the ball the same number of times, they measure the goal the same way, and they even shake hands for luck after every shot. All of this is by design, and it helps to breed confidence and consistency. Next time the NBA is on, study the best shooters from the free throw line and watch their habits.

They rarely change…

How long should a pre-shot routine take?

I don't believe there is any set in stone time for a pre-shot routine. Different shots will each pose unique situations that may range from easy to difficult.

However, I believe from the time you get out of the golf cart and arrive at your ball – the process should take no more than 45 seconds.

In fact, the USGA has outlined rules on the matter, and you can review those by visiting the following link:

http://www.usga.org/rules/competition_guidelines/Pace-of-Play-Policy/

Now that we have an understanding of the why, let's get to the how and build your own unique routine…

THE PSR FORMULA

Confidence is Queen and the Pre-Shot Routine is King for lowering scores. Having a solid routine will instill confidence and allow you to remove tension from your shots – giving you better results.

First what we want to do is create is a base for consistency. And that's what the pre-shot routine does.

If we just grab a club and look at the target and hit and then the next shot grab a club and take a few practice swings, maybe go right foot forward on setup, there's no consistency there. We want to do the same process and steps every time we play a shot.

To build an effective routine, Rich and I have narrowed down the steps for you to focus on. Here is our Pre-Shot Routine Formula:

1. Situational Analysis
2. Shot Visualization / Club Selection
3. Alignment / Setup
4. One Thought Only
5. Pull the Trigger

SITUATIONAL ANALYSIS

You've got to know the shot you want to hit if you are going to have success in golf. In order to form the right solution to the problem, we must take an assessment of our surroundings.

View this first step as a scientific experiment – we just want to gather the most important data so we can assess it and develop a solution.

You can come up with your own formula, but here's what I like to do personally:

#1 Check the lie.

Is the lie clean or in the rough? Knowing this will help me dictate what kind of ball position and swing angle I may need to take.

#2 Check the Stance.

Do I have a good stance? Rarely will you find a perfectly flat shot on the course. Even in the middle of a fairway, you are likely to have a bit of an incline or decline as well as an uphill or downhill stance – or even a combination.

Knowing the stance and how to setup properly for the situation will go miles in lowering your score. You can basically eliminate fat or thin shots by just taking notice of the stance you need to take.

#3 Check the Wind.

How strong is the wind? All we want to do here is gauge the wind in terms of MPH. This will allow you to use a little trick I've created to know how much to club up or down. I'll teach you my trick in the club selection phase, but for now, we just want to estimate the wind speed.

First, check the wind speed by scanning the top of the tree line. Second, you can even check your phone weather app for wind speeds.

What direction is the wind coming from for the shot you are about to play?

In my personal routine, I'm not too concerned about a slight breeze – I'm concerned about a brisk wind that is constant. Simply because a breeze isn't going to have much impact on my shot.

And we've all seen pro golfers grab a chunk of grass and throw it in the air. Usually, this is because the wind direction is not discernable because the winds are so light. I would advise against getting this anal about things… just because this is for tour caliber golfers who are playing a game of feet instead of yards.

As for variable winds, these can be tough… you just have to make a decision and be confident it's going the be the right one. My general rule of thumb here is to guess the wind gust, then factor in the frequency of the gusts. If it's not often, I will take my regular iron for the shot. Variable winds can often be swirling ones as well… and you can tell by looking at the top of the tree line and watching all of the trees swaying. You would then factor this into the style of shot you will play.

#4 Check for Trouble and Landing Zone.

Check the landing area for trouble spots. Are there bunkers in front or back? Is there a hidden creek over the hill that the course architect has skillfully hidden?

And most importantly, where do you want to land your shot? Ideally, I like to pick the highest percentage landing spot. I'm always thinking a shot ahead just like in pool. If I miss, I want to miss in an area where I can recover from with the highest chance of success.

In certain cases, I may elect to go for a green and risk a bunker. This is rare and to lower your score, you need to play the percentages. Chances are your game isn't as good as Adam Scott's.

#5 Check the Yardage.

Most of us today have yardage devices. Laser, GPS, and well marked courses have helped to virtually eliminate guessing.

I like to measure the yardage to the center of my landing zone – giving me a nice cushion surrounding the zone in case I miss the ball a bit.

NOTE: The situation analysis should take no more than 30 seconds to perform. Once you have all of the information at hand, it's time to visualize the shot you want to take.

SHOT VISUALIZATION / CLUB SELECTION

With every shot you almost always have 3 shots that can be played. And that's where the **3-Shot Rule** comes into effect. Generally, the 3-Shot Rule is something Rich and I use for trouble shots. However, it's a good practice to think outside the box and look at alternatives even for a straightforward shot.

#1 Visualize the Shot.

We want to give ourselves a lot of options here – ultimately with us deciding on the **HIGHEST CHANCE OF SUCCESS**.

Good golf can be quite boring – and you need to ensure you are making the best possible choice if you are serious about lowering your score.

The 3-Shot Rule comes into play when left with a difficult shot out of trouble or in a lie that isn't perfect (not to say this rule can't be played when sitting in the middle of the fairway).

What you want to do is identify the three shots you can play, ruling out the low percentage shots first and going with the high percentage shot.

What you'll find is the shot you really want to take is the high percentage one, which does not give you the best outcome.

Play these three shot options out in your mind, visualizing the ball flight, the roll, and even how the swing feels. Pick the shot that you are most comfortable with hitting. Comfort breeds confidence. Confidence helps eliminate tension.

Again, this should be a fairly quick process, maybe 10-15 seconds and you can do it while your playing partners are hitting their shots.

#2 Choose Your Club.

Once you have decided on the shot you wish to hit, it's time to take some of the data and pick our club.

Choose a Bulls-Eye Target and Safe Zone.

Choose a pretty decent sized area for your target and aim for the middle of it. This gives you a margin for error. I call this the **Safe Zone** and my rule of thumb is to pick a Bulls-Eye with a diameter of 20 yards around. This gives me a precise target and then a Safe Zone. And this gives me a very good chance of leaving myself a favorable next shot.

Next, you need to know the distance to the Bulls-Eye. I prefer to use a laser for precision, but you can use a GPS device as well. I'm looking for the sweet spot here where I want to land the ball. I'm looking for the safe play, the one that gives me a good chance at par or better. This will be the biggest, fattest area where I want my ball to land to give me the best chance at success for my next shot.

You should know how far you hit each club already. If you don't, head out to the range and assess every club in your bag and measure with a laser.

Once you have figured out the distance to the safe target zone, it's time to factor in the wind…

Factor the Wind.

My personal experience has taught me the **1 to 10 rule.**

Essentially, for every 10 MPH of wind I will either club up or down 1 iron. So if I have a backwind of 20MPH into a green that sets 150 Yards away, I will drop that club down by 2. So instead of an 8-iron, I go with a Pitching Wedge. Alternatively, if that wind were in my face, I would grab my 6-iron.

You will need to experiment on the range when it is windy to gather this data. Don't avoid golf on windy days, you can get extremely valuable data in windy conditions.

As for crosswinds, these are hard to judge and depend on your primary shot pattern. Do you draw or fade the ball? In these cases, use your best judgment, but aim to keep the ball landing in your target zone. Perhaps the wind is a right to left crosswind, so you should aim a bit more left than usual but still within the safe target zone.

Is a low shot (nice easy ¾ swing) going to give you better trajectory? Or do you want to play a high shot and let the wind carry it?

So now we know what type of shot we want to hit, we know our club, and we know our target zone. Now it's time to address the ball…

ALIGNMENT / SETUP

Knowing that we are setup properly gives us confidence. As we all know, confidence to hit a good shot is paramount to success in golf. We need to create a base for consistency.

This is the key really that we work for to build confidence. The confidence of knowing we are setup properly and the confidence of knowing the shot we want to hit. As Rich and I have said before, confidence will reduce tension and allow you to swing better.

My main focus on setup is to perform my setup exactly the same way for every club in my bag except for my driver. Essentially, I want to get lined up for the type of shot I want to hit so my ball lands in the target zone.

The great Jack Nicklaus would start his setup from BEHIND the ball. First visualizing his shot in his mind and then picking a spot roughly 5 to 6 inches ahead of the ball. He used this spot to line himself up when he got over the ball. I recommend you do the same.

He would step into the shot with his right foot with precision and then bring his left into his stance and offset it based on the club he was hitting. Setting up in this manner makes it almost fool proof. I suggest you give it a try as well.

Once you are setup over the ball and happy with your alignment, it's time to focus.

ONE THOUGHT ONLY

Standing over the ball, what do you think about?

If you are thinking about more than one thing, you are setting yourself up for disaster. I've heard some of the top players say they can focus on three things, but personally, this is just a bit too much. It's hard to focus your mind on more than one thing at a time. Especially in the short span of time it takes to swing a golf club.

Like Sands Through An Hourglass, So Should Be The Thoughts of Your Golfing Mind.

Only one grain of sand can pass through the neck of an hourglass. To calm our brains down and provide focus, we must provide all attention to ONE THOUGHT ONLY.

So let's focus on one thing and one thing only when we are standing over the ball. I'll bet money your game will improve. You WILL become more consistent.

Let's be clear, you should focus on what's working for you. We aren't on the course trying to fix our swing or work on new swing changes.

Some common swing thoughts Rich and I use are...

... *keep your eye on a dimple at the back of the ball.*
... *smooth takeaway.*
... *finish my backswing.*
... *sweeping takeaway, smooth along ground.*

Jack Nicklaus has suggested your swing thought for a smooth takeaway should be:

... *Ridiculously slow takeaway.*

It's best to develop your swing thoughts on the range when you are practicing. When you are striking the ball well, you need to ask yourself one question:

WHAT SWING THOUGHT IS WORKING RIGHT NOW?

One of the keys I have used to improve my own game has been taking notes after my practice sessions. If I was striking the ball well, or putting well, I wrote down exactly what I was thinking… ***and feeling***.

This one aspect alone has helped me smooth out my game on the course. One quick glance at my notes, and I can fix myself on the course. In fact, I used my notes when I was playing with a group of scratch golfers in South Carolina at TPC Myrtle Beach a few months ago.

I started topping my 3-wood, which is usually incredibly reliable. After three bad holes, I looked up my swing thoughts on my iPhone. I located some notes from when I was hitting my 3-wood well. I applied the swing thought on my next swing and hit a 300-yard laser down the middle.

In fact, Rich suggests you have more than one swing thought that works well for you. A round of golf is dynamic and flowing, just like our mind. Sometimes we can get off track and not know why. Having swing thoughts that we know work for us are immensely valuable.

A good swing thought is as good as money in the bank.

Having a notepad or an iPhone with a variety of swing thoughts can save your round. It's important to have just ONE SWING THOUGHT for each shot though.

I suggest you start 'saving' your good swing thoughts and building a substantial bank account you can withdraw from when needed.

Once you have your swing thought, it's time to…

PULL THE TRIGGER

Starting your backswing may sound super easy to the non-golfer, but as golfers, we know it can sometimes be the hardest part! Generally, this is a VERY personal situation, and one only you can address through practice.

Some golfers squeeze the grip or lift their heel up slightly before initiating the backswing. Jack Nicklaus used to turn his head to the right a split second before taking the club back.

Personally, I will begin my backswing with a tempo thought once I am COMFORTABLE over the ball. The key for me is **BEING COMFORTABLE**. If I don't feel good over the ball, I back away.

You should do the same. There's no reason to strike the ball with a bad feeling in your gut or with the wrong swing thought. You are just setting yourself up for a bad swing.

Rich usually combines his one thought with his takeaway movement, and almost always it is based on a smooth tempo. As a result, Rich has a beautiful golf swing and is rarely off tempo.

Pulling the trigger though is unique to each person and one you will most likely have developed already. Our suggestion is that you feel comfortable before initiating the backswing.

It's important to take notice of the top golfers in the world and learn from their experience. Tiger Woods is famous for backing away from a shot where he isn't confident or has been distracted.

Tiger simply begins his Pre-Shot Routine all over again from the start to finish.

Once you have developed a good PSR, you can use it to reduce pressure on the course through practicing smart. Rich and I will teach you how to do now...

To your best golf,

Christian Henning & Richard Guzzo
GOLFAGGRESSIVE.COM

HOW TO BREAK 90 IN 42 DAYS OR LESS

 ## Pre-Shot Routine

Week:
Date:

PRE-SHOT ROUTINE WORKSHEET

Description: Use this sheet to develop your own unique pre-shot routine.

A good routine takes time to perfect and will continue to evolve over your golf career. Use this worksheet to create a baseline and to also track changes you make. If you begin to start playing bad, it's a good idea to refer back to the routines you have tracked to ensure you are in check.

Have a friend time your routine from beginning to end as well. Try to keep things brisk, but not rushed.

PRE-SHOT ROUTINE

1.
2.
3.
4.
5.
6.
7.
8.
9.
10.

COMMENTS

Copyright © Golf Aggressive LLP.

ROBERT PHILLIPS

BONUS: HOW TO USE YOUR PRE-SHOT ROUTINE TO REDUCE PRESSURE

Practice like you play.

Pounding ball after ball on the range is NOT practicing like you play.

In fact, ball busting (as I like to call it) not only sounds painful, but it's probably hurting your golf game more than you know.

The underlying goal is to build consistency with your game, become repetitive at striking the ball perfect ALL the time…..and that only comes from a solid PSR (Pre-Shot Routine).

Take your time.

Golf isn't rocket surgery, but it's close! The key is to simplify the game over time and build in safeguards that help us play better during a round.

Practicing like we play does just that. Let me give you an example…

When I practice my putting, I start out by getting a feel for the green speed. I do this by striking three long putts downhill and then back uphill. I will then take those three balls and place them 10, 20 and 30 feet from the hole. I start at the 10 footer and move back.

Once I have a feel for the speed, I then start with 5 footers and listen for the ball to bang into the bottom of the cup to build confidence. After I've sunk about 5 or 6 in a row, it's time to play.

I put two balls into my bag and then play 18 holes. My goal is to 1 or 2-putt every hole and keep score.

This is where I go into my full putting routine that I use on the course. I read the green, take practice strokes, and even line the ball up at my aim point.

Another thing about this method, I don't pick easy holes… I present myself with a challenge. This helps to develop my game on two levels:

1. I can find weak points in my putting game. If I am lagging up within 4 to 5 feet but missing my knee knockers, I know what I need to

work on.
2. I learn how to deal with pressure. By keeping score on the putting green and going through my routine, I am preparing myself for battle.

To make this more challenging, compete against a friend for a beer. Anything you can do to build pressure will pay off during your competitive rounds.

The same can be done for your full swing shots. In fact, you can play an entire round right on the practice range and putting green. When I have prepared to play in tournaments I have sometimes taken practicing under pressure to extremes.

Luckily, my Country Club has a driving range directly next to the putting green. This allows me to play a 'golf course' without much work, while mimicking the variety of shots I might face.

For example, if it's a busy day at the course and I can't get a tee time, I will pretend that I am playing. I will tee up my driver for the first hole and swing. I pay attention to where it lands, then grab my 8-iron for my approach shot. If I strike it well and it hits the driving range green, I will grab my putter and head over to the putting green and try to hole out.

This gives me a full 18 holes I can play relatively quickly… all while keeping score. Sure, it's not as challenging as the real course, but you would be surprised at how fun and productive this can be for your game.

Challenge yourself and build pressure during your practice sessions – it will pay immense dividends for your score.

To your best golf,

Christian Henning & Richard Guzzo
GolfAggressive.com

ABOUT THE AUTHOR

At 48 years young, Robert routinely pounds the ball 300+ yards off the tee and can easily reach par 5's in two shots. With diligent and focused practice, he has whittled his handicap down from 20 to 10 over the past several years and routinely shoots score in the mid 80s.

ROBERT PHILLIPS

Printed in Great Britain
by Amazon